A Matter For Judgment

Globe Book Company, Inc.
New York/ Chicago/ Cleveland

A Matter For Judgment

Stories of Moral Conflict

Charles G. Spiegler
&
Roger B. Goodman

ACKNOWLEDGMENTS

We thank the following authors and companies for their permission to use copyrighted material:

BERNARD V. DEUTCHMAN—for "We Couldn't Let Him Die" adapted from a story in *The Haaren High School Liberator.* Adapted and published by permission of BernardV. Deutchman.

CARLA FINE—for "To Lie or Not To Lie" by Carla Fine. Adapted and published by permission of Carla Fine.

HOLT, RINEHART AND WINSTON, PUBLISHERS—for "The Lord Helpeth Man and Beast" from *The Jewish Caravan,* selected and edited by Leo W. Schwarz. Copyright 1935. © 1963, 1965 by Leo W. Schwarz. Reprinted by permission of Holt, Rinehart and Winston, Publishers.

HAROLD OBER ASSOCIATES INCORPORATED—for "The Enemy" by Pearl S. Buck. Copyright © 1942, 1947 by Pearl S. Buck. Copyright renewed 1969. Reprinted by permission of Harold Ober Associates Incorporated.

RANDOM HOUSE, INC.—for specified adaptation of "The Servant" by S. T. Semyonov from *Best Russian Short Stories* edited by Seltzer.

READER'S DIGEST SERVICES, INC.—for "The Lesson I'll Never Forget" by Edna Wilson Warren. Reprinted with permission from the May 1959 Reader's Digest (Teacher's Edition). Copyright 1959 by Reader's Digest Services, Inc. Reprinted and adapted by permission.

BEN AMES WILLIAMS, Jr.—for "They Grind Exceeding Small" by Ben Ames Williams. Adapted and published by permission of Ben Ames Williams, Jr.

The author wishes to state that every effort has been made to locate the following author or his heirs to obtain permission to reprint and adapt the following story: "Kong at the Seaside" by Arnold Zweig. If either the author or his heirs are located subsequent to publication, they are hereby entitled to due compensation.

Edited by David J. Sharp/Helen Breen
Illustrated by Marsha Cohen
Editorial/Production Services by Cobb/Dunlop, Inc.

Copyright © 1979 by Globe Book Company, Inc.
New York, N.Y. 10010
Published simultaneously in Canada by Globe/Modern Curriculum Press

ISBN: 0-87065-284-2

Printed in the United States of America
3-4-5-6-7-8-9-0

About the Authors

Charles G. Spiegler has been a teacher of English and speech in the New York City School System and Chairman of academic subjects for New York City Vocational Schools. He is the author and editor of numerous articles and books in the field of education. His work has appeared in such publications as *High Points, The New York Times Magazine, Parents' Magazine, NEA Journal, Reader's Digest,* and *The English Journal.*

Roger B. Goodman has been an English teacher in the New York City School System and for ten years was Chairman of the Department of English at Stuyvesant High School. His publications include *Masterpieces of World Literature, World's Best Short Short Stories,* and *World-Wide Short Stories,* published by Globe.

Contents

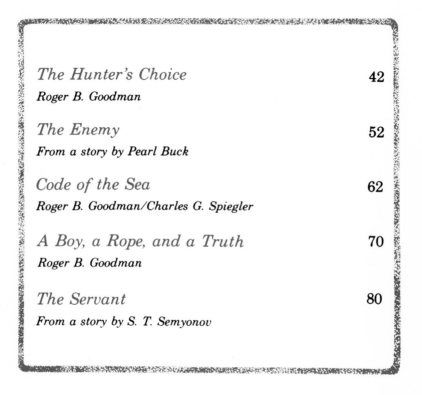

Contents

Poems for Thought

Introduction

Each story in *A Matter for Judgment* shows people in situations of conflict and moral choice. The story characters make decisions that have an important effect on their own life and the lives of others. Observe how each character handles a difficult situation. You may agree or disagree with the choice made by the characters. But in either case you will have the opportunity to deal with some of life's most challenging issues.

For instance, what would you do if you were a doctor in wartime and the life of an enemy prisoner were in your hands? Would you treat his wounds and risk punishment? Or would you turn him over to the authorities— and to an almost certain death?

If you see dishonesty in the business where you work, would you report it? Or would you go along with it in order to keep your job?

What if someone offered you a lot of money for a pet you loved. Would you accept the money and give up your pet? Or would you refuse the money? What things do you have that are worth more to you than money?

How much risk are you willing to take to help other people? What are you willing to give up in order to do what you think is right? What is your response to injustice when you see it? These and many other questions involving courage and responsibility, truth and injustice, right and wrong, are raised in *A Matter for Judgment*.

Following each story are activities that will help you sharpen your thinking and improve your reading. "Building Your Vocabulary" will help broaden your vocabulary, while "Understanding the Story" will give you practice in finding the main idea of a story, locating significant details, and using your reason to draw inferences. "You Be the Judge" is a discussion section that challenges you to consider each issue in light of your own beliefs and experiences. "Things To Do" includes oral and written activities that will increase your understanding of people and the world you live in.

Moral decisions—choices made in situations of conflict—are not easy to make. They often call for great courage, self-knowledge, and careful consideration of alternatives and outcomes. The stories and activities in *A Matter for Judgment* will give you a chance to do some hard thinking about values and what is truly important in your life.

This above all: to thine own self be true,
And it must follow, as the night the day,
Thou canst not then be false to any man.
SHAKESPEARE, Hamlet

Of all the crafts, to be an honest man is
the mastercraft.
JOHN RAY, English Proverbs

People of ill judgment oft ignore the good
That lies within their hands, till they have lost it.
SOPHOCLES

'Tis with our judgments as our watches, none
Go just alike, yet each believes his own.
ALEXANDER POPE

One falsehood spoils a thousand truths.
ASHANTI PROVERB

A Matter
For Judgment

The Lord Helps
Man and Beast

Traditional

Alexander the Great was born in 356 B.C. in Macedon, a kingdom north of Greece. His father was Philip II, king of Macedon. After his father was murdered, the 20-year-old Alexander became king. Philip's enemies started to take over parts of the kingdom, and Alexander set out to overthrow them.

Alexander succeeded beyond his original plans. Not only did he defeat his enemies at home, but he also conquered Persia and Egypt. His advisors wanted him to stop his conquests. But Alexander wanted to conquer Asia as well. To carry out this idea, Alexander led his troops from Africa to Afganistan and then into India.

People have made up many stories about Alexander. The following is a story that tells how one chief got the better of Alexander without a drop of blood being shed.

During his march of world conquest, Alexander the Great came to a people in a most distant and secluded corner of Africa. They were a peaceful people who knew nothing about war or conquerors. They led him to their chief's hut. The chief greeted Alexander in a friendly manner. Then the chief had his servants place before Alexander dates, figs, and bread made of gold.

"Do you eat gold in this country?" asked Alexander.

"No," replied the chief. "But I felt that you must have ordinary food in your own country. Why, then, would you come to mine?"

"I'm not tempted by your gold," laughed Alexander. "But I would like to study your manners and customs."

"You are welcome to stay with us as long as you like," said the chief.

Shortly after this conversation, two citizens entered. They had a legal problem that the chief would have to decide.

1

The first said, "I bought a piece of land from this man. As I was plowing it, I found a great treasure. This is not mine. When I bought the land, I did not bargain for anything that might be beneath it. But this man will not take the treasure from me."

The second man replied, "I hope my conscience is as strong as my neighbor's. When I sold him that land, I sold it to him with everything in and on it. And that includes the treasure."

Both men waited for the chief to render his decision.

He turned to the first man. "Friend, I believe you have a son. Right?"

"Yes."

"And you," turning to the other, "have a daughter?"

"Yes."

"Well, then," said the chief, "let your son and your daughter marry, and give them the treasure as a wedding present."

Alexander seemed surprised and perplexed.

"Do you think my judgment was unjust?" asked the chief.

"Oh, no!" replied Alexander. "But it astonishes me."

"Well, how would this case have been decided in your country?"

"To tell the truth," said Alexander, "we would have thrown both men into prison. Then the treasure would be seized for the king's use."

"For the king's use!" exclaimed the chief. "Tell me. Does the sun shine in your country?"

"Of course," said Alexander, puzzled again.

"And does it rain there?"

"Assuredly it does."

"Wonderful! And are there tame animals in your country that live on grass and green herbs?"

"Of course," said Alexander. "Very many of them. And of very many kinds."

"Ah," sighed the chief. "It must be for the sake of those animals that the All-gracious Being lets the sun shine and the rain drop down on your country. For certainly the people are unworthy of such blessings."

Alexander stood, silent and ashamed.

Building Your Vocabulary

1. The *conquest* of Mt. Everest took skill and courage. *Conquest* (p. 1) means (A) victory (B) record (C) settlement (D) debate
2. The cottage was built in a *secluded* spot in the woods near the lake. *Secluded* (p. 1) means (A) hidden (B) hot (C) lively (D) interesting
3. Because his *conscience* bothered him, Bill turned in the money he had found to the principal's office. *Conscience* (p. 2) means (A) pride (B) fun and humor (C) success (D) knowing right from wrong
4. When the jury came back into the courtroom, the foreman said, "We are unable to *render* a verdict of "not guilty." *Render* (p. 2) means (A) avoid (B) give (C) write (D) try
5. She was *perplexed* when she discovered that her cat was sitting in a tree. *Perplexed* (p. 2) means (A) bewildered (B) cheerful (C) calm (D) reassured

3

The Lord Helps Man and Beast

Understanding the Story

Choosing Another Title

1. Which title tells most about the story?
   (A) Kings and Peasants (B) The Golden
   Opportunity (C) The Chief's Mistake (D) The
   Conqueror Is Humbled

Finding Details

2. When Alexander is taken to the chief's hut, the
   chief is
   (A) angry (B) silent (C) friendly (D) asleep
3. Alexander is in Africa to
   (A) make a good-will visit (B) conquer that area
   (C) complete a trip around the world (D) hunt
   lions
4. Alexander tells the chief that he would like
   (A) something to eat (B) some gold (C) to study
   the customs of the country (D) to have a place to
   spend the night
5. The chief tells Alexander that he
   (A) is welcome to stay (B) can take what he wants
   (C) must leave a gift (D) must act as a judge
6. The problem between the two citizens involves
   (A) damage to property (B) friendship
   (C) a buried treasure (D) children
7. When the chief pronounces his judgment,
   Alexander says that he is
   (A) perplexed (B) astonished (C) sad (D) angry

Using Your Reason

8. When the chief gives Alexander gold instead of
   food, the chief is suggesting that Alexander

(A) has not come to a distant country to eat (B) has never seen such wealth (C) had better take the gold and leave (D) is foolish to continue his journey

9. The two citizens who come to the chief want to (A) get the gold (B) be honorable (C) outwit the king (D) steal some land

10. Alexander is ashamed because people in his country do not (A) have treasure (B) have weddings (C) enjoy the sun (D) act generously

You Be the Judge

1. What would your decision in regard to the treasure be if you were the chief?
2. How would you judge the chief's decision if you were the son or daughter? Explain.
3. If you bought a house and found something valuable in it that the previous owners had left, what would you do? Why?

Things To Do

1. Write down five things that if you found you would return immediately to the owner.
2. Write down five things that if you found you would keep.
3. Write a paragraph explaining your reasons for returning some things and not returning others.

Kong
at the Seaside

Arnold Zweig

This story is about money and what money can buy. Different countries have different types of money. In this story the English unit of money, the pound, is used. When you read this story, you will find out what 100 pounds can and cannot buy.

K ong got his first glimpse of the sea as he ran on the beach, which stretched like a white arc along the edge of the cove. He barked with enthusiasm. Again and again, the bluish-white spray came dashing up at him and he was forbidden to hurl himself into it! A tall order for an Airedale terrier with a wiry brown coat and shaggy forelegs. However, Willie, his young god, would not permit it; but at any rate he could race at top speed across the firm sand, which was still damp from the ebbing waters, Willie following with lusty shouts. Engineer Groll, strolling after, noticed that the dog and his tanned, light-haired, eight-year-old master were attracting considerable attention among the beach-chairs and gaily striped bathing-houses. At the end of the row some controversy seemed to be in progress. Willie was standing there, slim and defiant, holding his dog by the collar. Groll hurried over. People in bathing suits looked pretty much alike, social castes and classes intermingled. Heads showed more character and expression, though the bodies which supported them were still flabby and colorless, unaccustomed to exposure and pale after a long winter's imprisonment within the darkness of heavy clothing. A stoutish man was sitting in the shade of a striped orange tent stretched over a blue framework; he was bending slightly forward, holding a cigar.

"Is that your dog?" he asked quietly.

A little miss, about ten years old, was with him; she was biting her underlip, and a look of hatred for the boy and the dog flashed between her tear-filled narrow lids.

"No," said Groll with his pleasant voice, which seemed to rumble deep down in his chest, "the dog belongs to the boy, who, to be sure, is mine."

"You know dogs aren't allowed off the leash," the quiet voice continued. "He frightened my daughter a bit, has trampled her canals, and is standing on her spade."

"Pull him back, Willie," laughed Groll. "You're quite right, sir, but the dog broke away and, after all, nothing serious has happened."

Willie pushed Kong aside, picked up the spade and bowing slightly, held it out.

No one took the spade from the boy, and Willie, with a frown, stuck the toy into the sand in front of the girl.

"I think that squares it, especially on such a beautiful day," Groll smiled and lay down. Willie has behaved nicely and politely; how well he looks with his Kong. The dog, evidently not as ready to make peace, growled softly, his fur bristling at the neck; then he sat down.

"I want to shoot his dog, Father," the girl suddenly remarked in a determined voice; "he frightened me so." Groll noticed a gold bracelet of antique workmanship about her wrist—three strands of pale green-gold braided into the semblance of a snake. "These people need a lesson, I shall give it to them."

Groll nodded reassuringly at his boy, who was indignantly drawing his dog closer to him. The grown-ups seemed to know that the girl had the upper hand of them, or, as Groll told himself, had the right to give orders.

"No one is going to shoot my dog," threatened Willie, clenching his fists; but the girl continued:

8

"Buy him from the people, Father; here is my check-book." She actually took the thin booklet and a fountain-pen with a gold clasp from a zipper-bag inside the tent.

"If you won't buy him for me, I'll throw a soup plate right off the table at dinner; you know I will, Father." She spoke almost in a whisper and was as white as chalk under her tan; her blue eyes, over which the sea had cast a greenish glint, flashed threateningly.

The gentleman said: "Ten pounds for the dog."

"The dog is not mine; you must deal with my boy. He's trained him."

"I don't deal with boys. I offer fifteen pounds, a pretty neat sum for the cur."

Groll realized that this was an opportunity of really getting to know his son. "Willie," he began, "this gentle-man offers you fifteen pounds for Kong so he may shoot him. For the money, you could buy the bicycle you have been wanting since last year. I won't be able to give it to you for a long time, we're not rich enough for that."

Willie looked earnestly at his father, wondering whether he could be in earnest. But the familiar face showed no sign of jesting. In answer he put an arm about

9

Kong's neck, smiled up at Groll, and said: "I won't sell him to you, Father."

The gentleman in the bathing suit with his still untanned pale skin turned to Groll. Apparently the controversy began to interest him. "Persuade him. I offer twenty pounds."

"Twenty pounds," Groll remarked to Willie; "that would buy you the bicycle and the canoe, which you admired so much this morning, Willie. A green canoe with double paddles for the water, and for the land a fine nickel-plated bicycle with a headlight, storage battery, and new tires. There might even be money left over for a watch. You only have to give up this old dog by handing the leash to the gentleman."

Willie said scornfully: "If I went ten steps away, Kong would pull him over and be with me again."

Groll said, "You see, sir, the dog is a thoroughbred, pedigreed, and splendidly trained."

"We've noticed that."

"Offer fifty pounds, Father, and settle it."

"Fifty pounds," repeated Groll, and his voice shook slightly. That would pay for this trip, and if I handled the money for him, his mother could at last regain her strength. The sanatorium is too expensive, we can't afford it. "Fifty pounds, Willie! The bicycle, the watch, the tent —you remember the brown tent with the cords and tassels—and you would have money left to help me send mother to a sanatorium. Imagine, all that for a dog! Later on, we can go to the animal welfare society, pay three shillings, and get another Kong."

Willie said softly: "There is only one Kong. I will not sell him."

"Offer a hundred pounds, Father. I want to shoot that dog. I shouldn't have to stand such boorishness."

The stoutish gentleman hesitated a moment, then made the offer. "A hundred pounds, sir," he said huskily.

"You don't look as though you could afford to reject a small fortune."

"Indeed, sir, I can't," said Groll, and turned to Willie. "My boy," he continued earnestly, "a hundred pounds safely invested will within ten years assure you of a university education. Or, if you prefer, you can buy a small car to ride to school in. What eyes the other boys would make! And you could drive mother to market; that's a great deal of money, a hundred pounds for nothing but a dog."

Willie, frightened by the earnestness of the words, puckered up his small face as though to cry. After all, he was just a small boy of eight and he was being asked to give up his beloved dog. "But I love Kong and Kong loves me," he said, fighting down the tears in his voice. "I don't want to give him up."

"A hundred pounds—do persuade him, sir! Otherwise my daughter will make life miserable for me. You have no idea," he sighed—"what a row such a little lady can kick up."

If she were mine, thought Groll, I'd leave marks of a good lesson on each of her dainty cheeks; after glancing

11

at his boy, who, with furrowed brow, was striving to hold back his tears, he said aloud, quietly, clearly, looking sternly into the eyes of the girl. "And now, I think, the incident is closed."

Then a most astounding thing happened. The little girl began to laugh.

"All right, Father," she cried. "He's behaved well. Now we'll put the checkbook back in the bag. Of course, Father, you knew it was all in fun."

Building Your Vocabulary

1. The dog passed so quickly through the bushes that we only got a *glimpse* of its tail. A *glimpse* (p. 7) is a (A) shot at (B) brief look at (C) slight understanding of (D) strong hold on
2. A rainbow has many colors and is shaped in an *arc*. An *arc* (p. 7) is a (A) part of a circle (B) boat (C) square (D) house
3. They anchored the boat in a quiet *cove*. A *cove* (p. 7) is a (A) brook (B) inlet (C) river (D) dock
4. You can see the sunken ship only when the tide is *ebbing*. *Ebbing* (p. 7) means (A) moving fast (B) staying calm (C) going out (D) pounding
5. Willie was excited and gave *lusty* shouts. *Lusty* (p. 7) means (A) very energetic (B) frightened (C) angry (D) tearful
6. The *controversy* between the two men about the dog almost came to blows. *Controversy* (p. 10) means (A) a meeting (B) a sale (C) an argument (D) a friendly discussion
7. Willie was *defiant* because he wanted to keep his dog. *Defiant* (p. 7) means (A) disrespectful

12

(B) timid (C) not afraid (D) right
8. The rider spoke *reassuringly* to the startled horse and patted him on the neck. *Reassuringly* (p. 8) means (A) harshly (B) comfortingly (C) warningly (D) excitedly
9. Her *boorishness* and lack of caring caused her to have few friends. *Boorishness* (p.10) means (A) rude behavior (B) strong beliefs (C) soft voice (D) intelligence
10. The *earnestness* of the father's words showed that he meant what he said. *Earnestness* (p. 11) means (A) humor (B) seriousness (C) stupidity (D) meanness

Understanding the Story

Choosing Another Title

1. Which title tells most about the story?
(A) A Day at the Beach (B) The Well-Behaved Dog (C) The Dog Money Couldn't Buy (D) A Boy and His Dog Play Catch

Finding Details

2. According to the story, people in bathing suits look so much alike that it is difficult to tell the (A) men from the boys (B) rich from the poor (C) strong from the weak (D) city people from the country people
3. The boy in the story is described as being (A) tan with light hair (B) short with thick hair (C) tiny with clean hair (D) tall with wet hair
4. When Kong got his first glimpse of the sea, he

13

acted (A) frightened (B) confused (C) enthusiastic
(D) anxious
5. The girl said that if her father did not buy the
dog, she would
(A) not eat her supper (B) throw a soup plate
(C) scream and cry (D) jump up and down
6. According to the story, the boy's mother
(A) needed to go to a sanatorium (B) was away on
a trip (C) was home working (D) needed new
clothes
7. At the end of the story, the little girl treated the
whole incident as (A) an annoying matter
(B) a big joke (C) a serious business
(D) a terrible insult
8. Groll's attitude toward Willie was one of
(A) anger (B) pride (C) jealousy (D) annoyance

Using Your Reason

9. The girl's bracelet is mentioned to show that the
girl is (A) spoiled (B) wealthy (C) beautiful
(D) young
10. The action of the story shows that the girl's
money gives her the power to
(A) make everyone do anything she wants
(B) buy herself any dog (C) tease the man and his
son (D) have anything she wants

You Be the Judge

1. The boy Willie is offered money for his dog. This
money would give him some of the things he
wanted. What would you have done if you were
the boy? What would you have done if you were
the boy's father? Explain.

2. The story mentions that with the money for the dog, the boy's mother could go to a sanatorium and "regain her strength." Otherwise, she may continue to suffer because the "sanatorium is too expensive." Would this information change your decision about selling the dog if you were the son? If you were the boy's father? Why?

3. The boy's father allowed the girl to torment and tease his son because he "realized that this was an opportunity of really getting to know his son." What do you think of a father that would do this to an eight-year-old boy?

4. This story is partly about the way people who have power (the girl, the boy's father) are able to test or tease those who do not have power (Willie). What conclusions about life and people might Willie make from what happened to him?

5. If Willie had accepted the money for his dog, do you think the girl would really have given it to him? What do you think she would have done? Would this change the meaning of the story for you? How?

Things To Do

1. What kind of person is the little girl? Make a list of words that describe her. Write a paragraph describing what she might be like when she is grown-up.

2. Make a list of ways you might prevent people from teasing you. What can you do if somebody starts to tease you?

We Couldn't Let Him Die

Charles G. Spiegler

This story concerns five high school boys who rescue an old man. The story takes place in New York City. The author emphasizes how indifferent other people were to the old man. Do you feel that city life makes people harsh? Think about this question while you read the story.

It was rush hour in the subway when the old man fell. As he lay there unconscious and bleeding from the cut on his head, you'd think that what was lying there was an old newspaper, or a dirty rag, or a beaten-up jacket that someone threw away. Dozens of people saw him fall. Hundreds rushed by him after he fell. All they did was look at him stretched out on the subway station floor. They just kept on going. Nobody seemed to care whether he was bleeding to death—or even breathing.

Nobody, that is, except five high school students on their way to their first class. Sure, they were in a hurry like everyone else. "But how could I just let a guy lay there with all that blood coming out of his head ...?" asked one of the boys (Francisco Castro).

"Nobody paid any attention," said Luis Morales. "People just stepped over him and kept goin' like it was a dirty old coat you were stepping over. Jeez! He could have been stomped to death if we didn't step in."

This is how they described what they saw and felt and did, as the school newspaper, Haaren High School's *The Liberator,* reported it in an interview with the five boys:

17

We Couldn't Let Him Die

FRANCISCO CASTRO: I saw this old man fall. People in front of him just stepped aside and let him fall. He busted his head against the escalator steps . . . and, oh boy, I never saw so much blood. But nobody cared. Lots of people just stepped over him. Yeah, that's what I said. Just stepped over him . . . like it was a low hurdle in a race.

INTERVIEWER: You mean that nobody took a minute to. . . .

LUIS MORALES: Once in a while some people stopped—but just to watch. They surrounded him like this was a show or something.

MIGUEL PEDROZA: We even had a hard time getting through to him. One person got mad at me because I bumped into him on my way to the old man.

INTERVIEWER: Didn't they realize that the old man needed help?

MARTY FILOMENA: Maybe—but if they did, they didn't show it. They stood there like statues. And I'll tell you more. When we finally reached the victim, people looked at us as if we were trying to mug him.

INTERVIEWER: Mug him? You must be kidding.

LeROY SAXON: No . . . No kiddin'! That's the kind of looks we got. I guess everybody reads lots of stories about kids who mug old people. This is N.Y., and they don't expect kids to help an old man.

INTERVIEWER: So, how *did* you manage?

LUIS MORALES: We looked for a cop or a cab, but we couldn't see one. So we tried to get him on his feet to walk him to the hospital. That's only a block away, near the school. You know—Roosevelt Hospital.

MIGUEL PEDROZA: But a funny thing happened. He didn't want to go. "Take me to my daughter in the Bronx . . . she'll take care of me," he mumbled. But we insisted. So, we got him on his feet. He was staggering so bad, though, we practically had to carry him there.

MARTY FILOMENA: And you know what . . . people who passed

us ... they just kept walking. What did they think we were carrying—a stuffed animal?

FRANCISCO CASTRO: Well, anyhow, we got him into the Emergency Room just in time—just in time—that's what the doctor said. "Another twenty minutes and he could have bled to death." But he's OK now. We checked him out a few days later.

INTERVIEWER: Did you get to see him?

LEROY SAXON: Did we! And what a kick we got when we did. Even though we could hardly see his face—he had too many bandages all over his head—we heard his, "Thank you, thank you, boys. I'll never forget you for what you did for me." That was the best reward ... I mean it.

INTERVIEWER: The school is so proud of you fellows, you know that Mr. Deutchman (the Principal) is running an assembly in your honor.

* * *

At the school assembly, the spokesperson for the boys, Francisco, told the story again of how they had saved an old man's life. And the assembly cheered. But what seemed to make the greatest impact on the audience was the final statement the speaker made before he sat down. It went like this:

"The worst feeling I had during the whole time, was that the subway rider doesn't care about anything except going to work and coming from work as fast as he can— no matter who's in his way or what's happening around him. Even if someone were mugging that old man, most people would have just passed by."

Building Your Vocabulary

1. People rushed by so fast that they nearly *stomped* a man who had fallen down on the sidewalk. *Stomped* (p. 17) means (A) cut up (B) frightened (C) pressed underfoot (D) tore apart
2. After the boys had helped the old man cross the street, he *mumbled* his thanks. *Mumbled* (p. 18) means (A) forgot (B) jumbled (C) shouted (D) spoke in a low, unclear voice
3. Mr. Johnson, who had slipped on the ice, got up and *staggered* to his front door. *Staggered* (p. 18) means (A) walked unsteadily (B) walked very stiffly (C) walked with a firm step (D) ran in pain
4. To present their plan to the school assembly, the students chose Pedro as their *spokesperson*. A *spokesperson* (p. 20) is one who (A) argues (B) talks too much (C) speaks for others (D) speaks to express his or her own views
5. The action of Luis, Francisco, and their friends had an *impact* on the whole school. To have an

impact (p. 20) means to (A) make a great impression (B) have the power to hurt (C) have the need to hit or strike (D) want to argue

Understanding the Story

Choosing Another Title

1. Which title tells most about the story
   (A) Riding the Subways (B) A Trip to the Hospital
   (C) Juvenile Decency (D) A Day at School

Finding Details

2. The old man in the story fell
   (A) late at night (B) during a rush hour
   (C) on a Sunday afternoon (D) on a Saturday
   night
3. The five students stopped to help because they
   (A) were in no hurry (B) didn't want to go to
   school (C) felt they could be of service
   (D) had been learning first aid
4. The students at the school assembly were most
   impressed by the
   (A) bravery of the old man (B) speed with which
   the ambulance arrived (C) way the subway riders
   reacted (D) assistance given by the police
5. Francisco Castro became involved with the old
   man when he
   (A) accidentally brushed against him (B) saw him
   being mugged (C) asked him for some change
   (D) saw him fall
6. Luis Morales said that most of the people acted

as if the old man's accident was some kind of
(A) show (B) trick (C) joke (D) stunt

7. The old man was brought to the emergency room
by (A) a police officer (B) an ambulance
(C) five boys (D) several men

8. The old man thanked the boys by telling them
that he would
(A) never forget them (B) pay them some money
(C) talk to their principal (D) tell the newspapers

Using Your Reason

9. If the boys had not rescued him, the old man
might have died from
(A) a heart attack (B) fractured bones
(C) loss of blood (D) fever

10. According to the story, most people regarded the
old man as (A) a danger (B) an object (C) a hero
(D) a helper

You Be the Judge

1. People rushing to work may think that being on
time is important. Do you think that being on time
is important? Explain.

2. Why do you think the subway riders acted the way they did with regard to the old man?
3. If you were rushing to school for an important test, would you stop to assist someone? Explain.

Things To Do

1. Think of a time in your own life when you had the choice of helping someone in trouble or just minding your own business. What did you do? Are you glad or sorry you did it? Explain.
2. We read and hear much these days about how young people take advantage of the elderly. From your own experience describe instances that prove the opposite—young people who work with and for the elderly. Visit your library to learn about programs throughout the country that encourage students to serve the elderly.
3. Some communities reward citizens who have made sacrifices for the sake of others. In what way might the community reward the five students who helped this one old man? If you were asked to help make up a citation for these students, what would you write?
4. If the old man had been invited to speak to the assembly honoring the students who came to his assistance, what might he have said?

Prudence
Crandall

Roger B. Goodman

At the time of the American Revolution, most Northerners and Southerners favored a gradual end to slavery. But after the cotton gin was invented (1794) slavery became much more profitable. Slaves were needed to pick the cotton. The South then strongly defended slavery.

In the North antislavery feelings grew and more people worked to end, or abolish, slavery. This abolitionist movement was headed by William Lloyd Garrison, who founded the American Anti-Slavery Society in Philadelphia. The abolitionists helped slaves to escape from their masters and start a new life.

Prudence Crandall agreed with what the abolitionists said. She decided to open her school to black girls. Many people thought she was wrong to do this and they fought her. Today, because of people like Prudence Crandall, any child, regardless of color, has the right to an education.

For the first time, Prudence Crandall wept. She had not cried when the townspeople shouted insults at her and her students. She had not cried when the local children, encouraged by their parents, threw eggs at her and her students. She had not even cried when men armed with clubs broke all the windowpanes of her little school. But when they threw manure and dirt into her well, she broke down completely.

What crime had she committed? How could this bright, beautiful Connecticut town of Canterbury suddenly turn into a place of fierce and cruel monsters? And how could she, Prudence Crandall, a respectable, popular Quaker schoolmistress become so hated and despised?

In 1831 Prudence Crandall had opened the Canterbury Female Boarding School. It was a handsome, large building close to some of the best and wealthiest homes in

Canterbury. Actually it was right across the road from the home of Mr. Andrew T. Judson, a wealthy, powerful lawyer. He was one of those who had helped to establish the school. He had asked Miss Crandall to come to Canterbury as principal. Everyone in town was proud and happy about the new school. The daughters of all the best families in town went to Miss Crandall's school.

It was at just about this time in America that a man named William Lloyd Garrison started a movement called Abolitionism. The purpose of the Abolitionists was to abolish slavery immediately. They also wanted equal education for all people.

When Prudence Crandall heard about this movement, she became excited. She wanted to do something to help the cause of freedom. And something happened that gave her the opportunity.

A young black girl named Sarah Harris frequently came to visit Prudence's maid. Prudence found that Sarah was very bright and knew how to read and write. Sarah told Prudence that she wanted to be a school teacher. But she could not go back to school.

Prudence Crandall offered Sarah a place as a student in her school. And Sarah quickly accepted.

No sooner had this 17-year-old black girl begun attending classes than the town began buzzing. Very soon the parents of Miss Crandall's students took their daughters out of school. Most of the people in town couldn't understand why Miss Crandall was so stubborn. "All she has to do is get rid of that Harris girl," they said.

The people didn't know how determined and courageous Prudence Crandall really was. When she saw herself without any white students, Miss Crandall decided on a bold step. In February 1833 the local newspaper carried a simple announcement: "Beginning on the first Monday in April, The Canterbury Female Boarding School will be open for the reception of young ladies and little misses of color."

Then the storm broke over Prudence Crandall's head. Mr. Judson, Prudence's former friend, led a committee to see Miss Crandall.

"Miss Crandall," bellowed Mr. Judson, "you must stop this nonsense immediately. What are you trying to do to our town?"

"You are ruining the town!" shouted the mayor.

"If you don't stop right away," screamed the leader of a group of town mothers, "we'll find ways to deal with you."

But nothing could change Prudence Crandall's mind. She knew that she was right. And all of this occurred even before the new students had arrived.

The school did open on the first Monday in April 1833. The little girls who arrived from Boston, Providence, Philadelphia, and New York were, except for their color, just the same as the other little students. They were well-dressed, polite, and eager to learn. But the town saw them as only a threat. The protests now went beyond words.

The storekeepers in town refused to sell goods or food to Miss Crandall. The driver of the local stage refused to take the students or their parents as passengers. Even the town doctor and the minister of the local church refused to have anything to do with Miss Crandall or her students.

Local hoodlums went into action. They threw eggs and stones at the schoolhouse; they smeared mud over the walls, the windows, and the steps. And they dumped manure and filth into the school well. It was this that proved the final blow.

Several brave neighbors offered to help with food and transportation. But the obstacles were becoming too great. And Prudence Crandall was arrested for violating a newly passed "Black Law." This law made it illegal to educate colored persons who were not inhabitants of Connecticut. For refusing to obey this law, Prudence Crandall was sent to jail.

Some time later Miss Crandall decided to obey this Black Law. She sent home the little girls from out of state. But she still had almost 20 young black girls from Connecticut. And she continued to keep them in her school. Because of this, the abuses continued.

On July 22, 1834 the case against Prudence Crandall was dismissed. She hoped to be able to continue with her school without any trouble. But the school was attacked even more viciously. It was set on fire. And then, a few nights after the fire, a gang of men raided the school. They smashed every window in the building. This was the end. Prudence Crandall and the Reverend Calvin Philleo, whom she had recently married, left Canterbury and moved to New York.

Some years later, the State of Connecticut officially apologized to Miss Crandall. The State offered her a pension. The Black Law disappeared. Connecticut became one of the first states in the Union to grant full freedom to the blacks.

Perhaps, at first, Prudence Crandall's battle was lost. But in the end her war was won.

Building Your Vocabulary

1. When Miss Crandall made a decision, she was *committed* and did not back down. *Committed* (p. 25) means to be (A) happy (B) bound to something (C) patient (D) afraid to leave
2. Mr. Garrison wanted to *abolish* the law that permitted slavery. *Abolish* (p. 26) means to (A) favor (B) escape from (C) do away with (D) ignore

Prudence Crandall

3. The principal *bellowed,* and the student jumped
   out of her seat. *Bellowed* (p. 27) means
   (A) shouted (B) kept his voice low
   (C) spoke for a long time (D) bored the audience
4. Miss Crandall faced many *obstacles* in trying to
   keep her school open. *Obstacles* (p. 28) are
   (A) interferences (B) goals (C) opponents
   (D) warnings
5. The *inhabitants* of the town tried to destroy the
   school. *Inhabitants* (p. 28) are (A) people guilty of
   bad habits (B) residents (C) landlords
   (D) shopkeepers

Understanding the Story

Choosing Another Title

1. Which title tells most about the story?
   (A) Prudence Crandall Opens a School
   (B) Prudence Crandall: Typical Schoolteacher
   (C) How Prudence Crandall Stuck to Her
   Principles (D) How Prudence Crandall Went to
   New York

Finding Details

2. The first time Prudence Crandall wept in this
   story was when
   (A) eggs were thrown at her (B) the school
   windows were broken (C) she left for New York
   (D) manure and dirt were thrown into her well
3. Prudence Crandall noticed that Sarah Harris
   (A) had thrown eggs at the school (B) was very

30

bright (C) was homeless (D) needed clothes
4. When Prudence Crandall met with opposition,
   she was
   (A) determined and courageous (B) scared and
   timid (C) angry and anxious (D) depressed and
   discouraged
5. Andrew T. Judson was a man who
   (A) asked Prudence Crandall to be principal
   (B) was always opposed to the school (C) started a
   movement to abolish slavery (D) apologized to
   Miss Crandall
6. The Canterbury Female Boarding School was
   located in a town in
   (A) Ohio (B) Georgia (C) Colorado (D) Connecticut
7. Which method did the people of Canterbury NOT
   use to change Prudence Crandall's mind?
   (A) Storekeepers refused to sell her goods.
   (B) The stage driver refused to provide service to
   her students. (C) Hoodlums beat her students
   with clubs. (D) Children threw eggs at her and at
   her students.
8. The State of Connecticut put Prudence Crandall
   in jail and some years later
   (A) took all her belongings (B) officially apologized
   (C) rebuilt her school (D) asked her to come back

Using Your Reason

9. Henry David Thoreau went to jail to protest the
   Mexican-American War. He is like Prudence
   Crandall in that both (A) wrote books about their
   experiences (B) were schoolteachers who believed
   in justice (C) were willing to suffer for causes they
   believed were right (D) had their houses set on
   fire by mobs

31

10. Which sentence tells the saddest part of this story? (A) "But nothing could change Prudence Crandall's mind." (B) "The state offered her a pension." (C) "She sent home the little girls from out of state." (D) "Several brave neighbors offered to help ..."

You Be the Judge

1. Prudence Crandall had the courage to do what she believed was right. She believed it was right to obey the law. And she believed it was right that all people be able to go to school. At first Miss Crandall disobeyed the law and went to jail. Later she obeyed the law by sending her students back to their home states. What do you think is the right thing to do when you feel a law is unjust? How might you change a law in a peaceful way?

2. Prudence Crandall stood up for her beliefs no matter what other people did or said. Do you think it would have been a good idea for her to have compromised and given in a little to the wishes of the community? What would have been the outcome? When is it best to stand firm for what you believe? When is it best to give in? Explain.

Things To Do

1. Imagine that the State of Connecticut was having a statue made in honor of Prudence Crandall. There is room at the base of the statue for 100 words explaining why she is being honored. What would you write, if you were asked?

2. Find another example of a person who stood firm
    in what he or she believed regardless of the
    consequence. Explain what that person believed.
    Tell what happened to the person.

A
Play Review

Charles G. Spiegler

What you see is not what you get.

Find out how this saying applies to the following story.

Last night at the Starlight Theatre, I had the doubtful "privilege" of watching a musical comedy with music by Rex Biloxi. The book was by James Lackned, one of musical comedy's great lyricists. The play was called "The Moon is Up"! It is not, I'm afraid, anything Biloxi will look back upon with pleasure. The sooner he (and the public) forget it, the better.

The story line is simple indeed. A boy (Jimmy Blau), handsome, rich and idle, falls in love with a girl (Sally Conway). The girl is a beautiful and poor waitress in an all-night diner. He wants to marry her. She's in love with another man (Ted Sikorsky). The other man is a gas-station attendant who goes to night school. He is studying to become a computer operator. The songs are bad but the singers sing them with great gusto and talent. The lyrics are "blah" and dull. The audience gets no opportunity to stay awake to see what's going to happen next. Not much does anyway. Lackned is a talented writer, and he does have some magnificent lines in this musical. There is a whole section filled with truly hilarious jokes. But, as a whole, "The Moon is Up" is a disaster!

"Down" should have replaced "Up" in the title, except that then the authors might have been sued by the owners of John Steinbeck's "The Moon is Down."

35

Lackned and Biloxi have problems enough without being sued for plagiarism.

If, however, you enjoy a very realistic stage set (the all-night diner is absolutely perfect), you'll get a kick out of "The Moon is Up." If your eyes enjoy looking at beautiful people (the leading performers and the chorus line are just that), you'll appreciate "The Moon is Up." If you enjoy hearing fine voices (and they're here in abundance), you'll be glad you went to the Starlight. But if you're not willing to shell out money for a book that might have been written by a ten year old, and if you are not interested in listening to songs that put you to sleep, save your money for a good dinner in a diner.

* * *

The day after this review was published, the following advertisements appeared on the theater pages of many newspapers. The review you have just read was quoted as follows:

Go see "The Moon Is Up" with the lyrics of Rex Biloxi, "One of musical comedy's great lyricists"!
Charles Spiegler

Go see "The Moon Is Up." "It has a story line which is simple...". The singers perform "with great gusto and talent."
Charles Spiegler

By a "talented writer" who "has some magnificent lines, even a whole section filled with hilarious jokes."
Charles Spiegler

YOU'LL GET A KICK OUT OF IT!
Charles Spiegler

Building Your Vocabulary

1. The *lyricist* seemed unable to rhyme anything but moon, June, and soon. A *lyricist* (p. 35) is a person who (A) arranges music (B) creates dances (C) designs sets (D) writes words for songs
2. The actors all played their parts with *gusto*. *Gusto* (p. 36) means (A) sadness (B) enthusiasm (C) doubt (D) hope for approval
3. The audience laughed loudly at several *hilarious* scenes in the play. *Hilarious* (p. 36) means (A) funny (B) long (C) sad (D) active
4. Writers and lyricists must be careful not to commit *plagiarism*. *Plagiarism* (p. 36) is the act of (A) changing someone's words (B) erasing someone's words (C) covering up someone's words (D) stealing someone's words
5. The stage set showing a crowded bus station was very *realistic* because it looked like a real station. *Realistic* (p. 36) means (A) lifelike (B) ugly (C) dreamlike (D) comical

Understanding the Story

Choosing Another Title

1. Which title tells most about the play review? (A) A Play Worth Seeing (B) How To Write a Play Review (C) A Play Is Publicized (D) The History of Musical Comedies

Finding Details

2. The author of the play review says that he

37

watched the musical at the
(A) Biloxi Theater (B) Starlight Theater
(C) Steinbeck Theater (D) Towne Theater

3. According to the review, one of musical comedy's
    great lyricists is (A) Jimmy Blau (B) John
    Steinbeck (C) James Lackned (D) Dan Smathers
4. In the play Sally Conway performs the role of
    (A) musician (B) waitress (C) computer operator
    (D) writer
5. The review does NOT praise which of the
    following:
    (A) beautiful performers (B) realistic stage set
    (C) performers' fine voices (D) music and lyrics
6. The action of the play takes place in
    (A) a living room (B) an all-night diner
    (C) a city apartment (D) a park

Using Your Reason

7. The play's story line involves
   (A) a romantic triangle (B) a case of mistaken identity (C) a crime of passion (D) a king's thrust for power
8. All the praise in the ads comes from
   (A) an ad writer's mind (B) the review itself
   (C) the writer of the play (D) people who have not seen the play
9. The main idea of this selection is that
   (A) most plays are worthless (B) ads are generally honest (C) reviewers don't even watch the play
   (D) advertisements distort the truth
10. If the person who wrote the review were to rate plays from 0–10, with 10 being the highest rating, he would give this play (A) 0 (B) 3 (C) 8 (D) 10

You Be the Judge

1. What, if anything, is wrong with the advertisements for "The Moon Is Up"?
2. Do the people who invest money in putting a play on the stage have the right to protect their investment in any way possible?
3. Are the ads here examples of "false advertising"? How would you answer the writers of the ads if they argue, "We took words right from the review."?

Things To Do

1. Read a play, movie, or TV show review. Then

compare the review with advertisements for that event. Decide whether the advertisements are, at least in the reviewer's opinion, accurate.

2. If you can manage to see the play, movie, or TV show, decide whether you agree with the reviewer and/or the advertiser, or with neither.

3. Write a review of a play, movie, or TV show you have seen. Write the ads or commercials you would like to see in print or on the air.

4. Study the advertising section of your newspaper for any one day. Of all the products advertised, find one (or more) you have bought and used. Decide whether or not the ad for that product is accurate.

5. Think of suggestions you could make to the consumer agencies in your community to develop a

"Truth in Advertising" campaign. Write a letter offering your suggestions.

6. Get a piece of typing paper. Start tearing the paper. Keep tearing the paper, but don't tear it apart. After you have made a tear, twist the paper into any shape you want. Then staple the ends together. Now, imagine a rich person wants to sell thousands of the things you just made. The rich person wants you to give the thing a name and write an advertisement that will make people want to buy it. Think of a name and write an advertisement that will make people want to own the thing themselves.

The
Hunter's Choice

Roger B. Goodman

Eskimo villages are usually made up of five or six families and seldom have more than 40 people. One chief is appointed. Good hunters become leaders by virtue of their success. When they fail, they fall back, and others take their place.

Since World War II, groups of people with machinery and weapons have come into the arctic where Eskimos live. These people have destroyed much of the Eskimo's way of life.

This story tells of a group of people who, for what they believe is a "good cause," try to change the way one group of Eskimos lives.

Maluk, Eskimo hunter, sat quietly in his boat. He hardly dared to breathe. All around him everything was still. The ice floes were still and cold in the water. The sky was clear and blue above. The water seemed like glass. Right in front of Maluk was a great, grey object. It looked like a huge rock jutting out of the water. But Maluk knew it was a large whale resting. The faint spray from its nostrils showed that the whale was breathing peacefully.

Maluk's heart was pounding. He wanted to harpoon and kill this whale. It would mean food and clothing for many in his village. His father, Omook, a great hunter, lay sick in his igloo. And Maluk, hunting alone for the first time, wanted to succeed.

So slowly that he hardly seemed to move, Maluk picked up his heavy harpoon. It was almost 12 feet long. There was a sharp point on the end. Maluk wanted to strike the whale in the right place. If he missed, the whale would be frightened away and it would plunge to the bottom of the sea. If he came home empty-handed, he was afraid that people would laugh at him. "The great hunter Omook has no son," they would say. And Maluk would feel terrible.

Maluk was so close now that he could hear the whale's

43

breath. He stood up in his flat-bottomed boat, or umiak. He drew back his arm to strike.

Suddenly there was a roar from the sky. A helicopter swept down over Maluk and the whale. It had a big glass bubble and was painted red. Maluk looked up, startled.

The whale gave a great snort and with a flap of its huge tail plunged under the icy water. Maluk was trembling with rage. He shouted and shook his harpoon at the helicopter furiously. He was so angry he was nearly crying. The machine made one more circle. Then it began to fly in the direction of Maluk's village. Paddling furiously, Maluk turned to chase it.

About an hour later Maluk arrived at his village. He could see all the people standing in the big clearing in front of his igloo. They were talking and pointing at the helicopter that was now standing on the snow. In the middle of the crowd were three men. They were talking to the people. When the crowd saw Maluk, they all turned and waved to him.

But Maluk was more angry than he had ever been. He drew his boat up to the shore and jumped out. Then,

waving his harpoon over his head and shouting with rage, he ran toward the machine. He intended to smash the machine. But just as he got near it, one of the strange men stepped forward.

"Wait, Maluk," the man called. "We are friends. We want to talk to you."

Maluk stopped still and lowered his harpoon. "Friend? Why did you frighten my whale? Where will we get our food now?" he shouted.

"We have brought food, Maluk," said the man. "And we have brought clothing. And medicine for your father. But we must talk to you."

Maluk was astonished. "Well," he said, "talk."

"We are from an organization called the United Nations. And we are trying to save the whales from being killed off. Soon there will be no more whales. And that will be a terrible thing. Don't you think so?"

"It will be a terrible thing, surely," said Maluk. "But do you think that if I kill one whale a year—to feed my people and give them clothes—I will make all the whales disappear? I think you are foolish."

"What you say is true," answered the tall man. "But there are hunters in great boats with harpoon cannons. They kill off many whales in one year. And that is why we try to stop them."

Maluk made a face. He twisted his head around. "Do you see any cannon here?" he asked. "Do you see the bodies of many whales? Do you see the body of even one whale? Why don't you stop the hunters with the great boats?" asked Maluk. "I don't think they use the whole whale the way we do. Tell *them* to stop hunting. Then it won't be so hard for me."

The man looked down at his feet. His two friends came up to him and said something.

"Look," said the man. "I know that what you say is true. And I don't like to stop you, but ..."

45

"If you don't like it, then don't do it," said Maluk. "I agree that it will be a hard thing if all the whales disappear. But I don't think when I kill one whale, all the whales will vanish. I want to help your organization if I can. But I don't want people flying here with clothes and food when we can get our own. We have been independent for many years. We were independent in my father's time and in his father's time. And it is good. Is there a law in your organization against people taking care of themselves?"

"Well, yes. There is a law protecting the whale. And all the nations agree to it. That is why we are here," the man answered.

Maluk thought for a moment. "I did not make the law, nor did any of my people. I did not choose the people who made this law. Should I obey a law that is forced on us by strangers—a law that will destroy our way of life?"

The man was about to answer when he heard the radio from the helicopter. The man ran back to listen. When he returned, he seemed puzzled.

"I have to go now," he said. "It is my duty to tell you that it is illegal for you to hunt the whale." He hung his head. "I am very sorry, Maluk. I do not wish your people any harm."

Then he and his friends got back into the machine and, with a great roar and whirling of blades, they rose into the air and flew off.

Maluk and the villagers watched the machine go. They were all silent. Some of them held in their hands clothing the men had brought. But it was Maluk who had the great problem.

What must he do? The organization was right, he thought, in trying to save the whales. But what was he to do to bring food and clothing to his people? It is difficult, he thought, to be a hunter. And he now had to make a most difficult decision.

Building Your Vocabulary

1. The steel *harpoon* cut deeply into the side of the whale. *Harpoon* (p. 43) is used for (A) hunting (B) lifting (C) eating (D) sailing
2. Waving his harpoon *furiously,* he rushed at the machine. *Furiously* (p. 44) means (A) angrily (B) joyfully (C) drunkenly (D) hopelessly
3. The sudden appearance of the flying machine surprised and *astonished* him. *Astonished* (p. 45) means (A) scared (B) amazed (C) worried (D) delighted
4. The people got together and formed an *organization* whose purpose was the protection of animals. An *organization* (p. 45) is (A) a family (B) a trade agreement (C) a group (D) an understanding
5. The noise frightened the whale and caused it to dive and *vanish* beneath the sea. *Vanish* (p. 46) means to (A) disappear (B) snort (C) swim fast (D) leap

Understanding The Story

Choosing Another Title

1. Which title tells most about the story?
   (A) Maluk and the Whale Law (B) Maluk Catches
   a Whale (C) Maluk Protects the Whales
   (D) Maluk Feeds the Village

Finding Details

2. One reason Maluk knew that the large object in
   the water was a whale was that
   (A) it was colored blue (B) it made a high sound
   (C) a faint spray came from its nostrils (D) its tail
   splashed in the water
3. Maluk was afraid that if he did not kill the whale
   (A) people would laugh at him (B) it would injure
   people (C) it would tip over his boat (D) someone
   else would kill it
4. Maluk started to harpoon the whale when he was
   close enough to
   (A) touch it (B) see its eyes (C) hear its breath
   (D) feel it moving
5. When Maluk arrived home, the villagers
   (A) refused to talk to him (B) shouted at him
   (C) turned and waved to him (D) ran up and
   hugged him
6. The people in the helicopter did *not* bring which
   of the following
   (A) food (B) medicine (C) clothing (D) tools
7. The people in the helicopter were
   (A) tourists (B) hunters (C) United Nations
   representatives (D) coast guard sailors

8. Maluk's position in the community was that of
   (A) chief (B) hunter (C) warrior (D) captain

Using Your Reason

9. The most unlikely or absurd idea presented in the
   story is the idea that
   (A) a helicopter would scare off a whale (B) one
   man would go out alone in a boat to catch whales
   (C) whales could disappear from the earth
   (D) Maluk would argue with the men in the
   helicopter
10. The men from the helicopter and Maluk agree
    that killing
    (A) one whale will not make whales vanish
    (B) one whale is not illegal (C) whales is the best
    thing for Maluk to do (D) whales is an exciting
    sport

You Be the Judge

1. In the story Maluk is asked by the people from the
   United Nations not to kill whales. Do you think
   this is a reasonable request? Explain.
2. What would you have said to the men in the
   helicopter if you had been in Maluk's situation?
   What would you have done after they left?
3. One reason the American Colonies fought against
   Great Britain was that they objected to "legislation
   without representation." That means they did not
   like other people making laws for them to obey. Do
   you think the situation of Maluk in this story is
   similar to that of Colonial Americans? Explain.

Things To Do

1. Write a law that you think is fair and just and will protect the whales from being killed off.
2. Pretend you are Maluk and write a letter to the United Nations explaining your situation and what you are going to do.

To My Friend

Anonymous

I will not say to you, "This is the Way; walk in it."
For I do not know your way or where the Spirit may call
    you;
It may be to paths I have never trod or ships on the sea
    leading to unimagined lands afar,
Or haply, to a star!
Or yet again
Through dark and perilous places racked with pain and
    full of fear
Your road may lead you far from me or near—
I cannot guess or guide, but only stand aside.
Just this I'll say:
I know for every truth there is a way for each to walk, a
    right for each to choose, a truth to use.
And though you wander far, your soul will know that true
    path when you find it.
Therefore, go!
I will fear nothing for you day or night!
I will not grieve at all because your light is called by some
    new name;
Truth is the same!
It matters nothing to call it star or sun—
All light is one.

The Enemy

Pearl Buck

Sometimes in life there is a conflict between loyalties. In this story a Japanese doctor must choose between his loyalty to Japan and his loyalty to his profession as a healer. Read this story and find out which choice he makes.

"He's a white man," whispered Hana.

"And he is very badly wounded," muttered her husband, Dr. Sadao Hoki.

They stood silently on the seashore, looking down at the man motionless on the sand. An old sailor's hat was stuck on his head, soaked with sea water. His soaked clothes were in rags. The sand on one side of him already had a stain of blood soaking through.

Dr. Sadao Hoki's house was located along the coast of Japan. During this time of war, Dr. Hoki had been permitted to remain in Japan because of his discovery of a new technique for cleaning battle wounds. And the old General who had retired to the neighborhood was depending upon Dr. Hoki's skill to treat his own ailment.

As he looked down upon this wounded young man, Dr. Hoki knew that he was an escaped American prisoner of war. He knew that he was an enemy. Actually, Dr. Hoki knew quite a bit about America. He had studied in an American university. And it was at that university that he had met the young lady who was now his wife. So he had mixed feelings about the United States. All of his learning had come from there. The great love for his wife

53

had been born there. But now, and for the past few years, the United States had been an enemy land. And all Americans were his foes. Even this badly wounded young boy lying on the beach.

"What shall we do with this man?" Sadao muttered. As he bent over the unconscious form, Sadao's hands, almost with a will of their own, were probing the deep wound in the boy's back. "It would be best if we put him back into the sea."

"Yes," agreed his wife.

"If we shelter a white man in our house, we can be arrested. If we turn him over as a prisoner, he will surely die."

"Yes," whispered his wife.

"If he were well," continued Dr. Hoki, as though talking to himself, "I would not hesitate a minute to turn him over to the police. But since he is wounded ..."

"I know," murmured his wife.

Suddenly, Dr. Hoki stooped down and lifted the unconscious young American sailor into his arms. "We must take him to the house."

As Dr. Hoki carried the young enemy into his house, he saw the eyes of his servants. They were hostile and angry.

"The master ought not to heal the wound of this white man," said the old gardener. "The white man ought to die. If the master heals him, we will all be punished."

But Dr. Hoki seemed to hear nothing anyone said. He had the sailor's clothes cut off, and, since the servants refused to have anything to do with their enemy, he had Hana, his own wife, wash the thin, almost starved young man. And he asked her to help him with the operation he knew he had to perform.

While Dr. Hoki was performing the operation, the young man groaned with pain.

"Groan," Dr. Hoki muttered, "groan if you like. I am not doing this for my own pleasure. In fact, I do not know why I am doing it."

It was the next day. The operation had been successful. And, amazingly, the young man, weak and badly wounded as he was, began to improve. When he woke up from his long sleep, he saw Dr. Hoki's wife. A look of fear came into his eyes.

"Don't be afraid," she said softly.

"How come you speak English?" gasped the young sailor.

"I was a long time in America," she explained. "Now rest some more."

Later on, when the wounded man had recovered enough of his strength to sit up, Dr. Hoki went to see him.

"What are you going to do with me?" the boy muttered. Dr. Hoki felt that he could be no more than seventeen. "Are you going to turn me over?"

"I do not know what I shall do with you. I should give you up to the police. You are a prisoner of war—no, do not tell me anything." Dr. Hoki put up his hand to stop the boy from speaking. "Do not even tell me your name."

"OK," the boy whispered, his mouth a bitter line.

Time passed. The boy grew stronger. He was soon well enough to walk around his room. He even became cheerful and wanted to talk to Dr. Hoki and his wife. But Sadao and Hana did not want to enter into discussions with him. Dr. Hoki knew he couldn't keep the boy in his house much longer. He wanted to do what was right. He wanted to turn him over to the police. But he kept having doubts and questions in his mind.

Finally, he made up his mind. He went to the boy's room.

"You are well now," he said. "You are so well that if I put my boat on the shore, with food and extra clothing, you might be able to row to that little island not far from the coast. Tonight. You must leave tonight. There is nobody on the island. You could live there until you saw a Korean fishing boat pass by."

The young man stared at him, slowly beginning to understand. "Do I have to?" he asked.

"I think so," Sadao answered, gently. "You are not safe here."

Later that evening, Dr. Hoki went to the American's room. The boy was waiting impatiently.

"I realize that you are saving my life again," he said.

"Not at all," said Dr. Hoki, "It is only inconvenient to have you here any longer."

Then, giving the boy his own flashlight, he said, "When you get to the island, if you are all right, use this flashlight to signal me once."

"OK," the young man breathed. Then, without a word, he reached over and shook Sadao's hand warmly. And he stepped into the darkness.

Dr. Hoki waited for a long time. Then, through the darkness, he saw one flash. After that he closed the partitions of the house. For the first time in several nights, he slept well.

There was no news of any kind for several days, and then for a week. Dr. Hoki knew that the young man had been rescued. Thoughts flashed through his mind of his stay in America. He recalled his fat sloppy landlady who had resented his even renting a room in her house. He remembered the silly, chattering wife of his dull professor at the University. He remembered how unhappy he had been surrounded by all those white faces. He almost felt a sense of relief that Japan was openly at war with them and their country. Then he recalled the youthful, haggard face of his prisoner—white and repulsive.

"Strange," he thought. "I wonder why I could not kill him."

Building Your Vocabulary

1. Doctors are always looking for new and better *techniques* to treat diseases. *Techniques* (p. 53) are (A) preventions (B) methods (C) purposes (D) needs

2. During World War II when the United States was at war with Japan, many Americans felt *hostile* toward Japanese Americans. *Hostile* (p. 55) means (A) unfriendly (B) annoyed (C) upset (D) frightened
3. My father and mother built a *partition* in our attic to make two extra bedrooms. A *partition* (p. 56) is (A) a widening (B) a division (C) a tearing down (D) an improvement
4. After his long illness, the sailor felt stronger but still looked pale and *haggard*. *Haggard* (p. 57) means (A) young (B) fat (C) red (D) worn out
5. I think snakes are *repulsive*, but my friend Leo keeps two as pets. *Repulsive* (p. 57) means (A) brave (B) exciting (C) pleasant (D) disgusting

Understanding the Story

Choosing Another Title

1. Which title tells most about the story? (A) All's Fair in Love and War (B) A Common Humanity (C) Blood Is Thicker Than Water (D) War Is for Heroes

Finding Details

2. Judging from Dr. Hoki's discovery and the fact that the old general wanted him around, we can conclude that the general was suffering from (A) old age (B) battle wounds (C) diabetes (D) a bad diet

3. The doctor didn't let the American die because
   the doctor
   (A) was an American citizen (B) liked Americans
   (C) had been treated well as an American student
   (D) believed his duty as a doctor was to save lives
4. At first the doctor wanted to throw the wounded
   man back into the sea because
   (A) he had no medication to offer (B) he feared
   discovery (C) the sailor wanted no help (D) the
   doctor's wife wanted to protect her husband
5. The servants refused to help the doctor because
   they (A) were superstitious (B) feared punishment
   (C) wanted to keep their hands clean (D) hated all
   foreigners
6. How did the doctor's wife behave?
   (A) She argued with her husband. (B) She always
   stayed in the kitchen. (C) She helped her
   husband. (D) She gave excuses for her husband.
7. The wounded American was
   (A) a doctor (B) a prisoner of war (C) an aviator
   whose plane had fallen into the sea (D) a tourist
   whose ship had been sunk
8. During the operation, the doctor
   (A) had doubts as to why he was doing it (B) had
   pleasure in hurting an enemy (C) had doubts that
   the man would survive (D) worried that he'd be
   caught saving an enemy

Using Your Reason

9. When the doctor brought the American home, the
   old gardener felt
   (A) relieved (B) scared (C) glad (D) indifferent

59

10. At the end of the story, the doctor "slept well" because he was
(A) certain he did the right thing (B) glad that he was a doctor (C) sure his good deed would get back to the old general (D) no longer in such danger

You Be the Judge

1. The Japanese doctor was not loyal to the laws of his country by helping a prisoner escape. Do you think people should always obey the law? Do you think there are any exceptions? If so, under what circumstances do you think it is right to break the law?
2. What would you think of an American doctor that treated an enemy and helped him escape? What do you think the United States government would do to the doctor if they found out about it? Do you think there is any difference in this situation and the one in the story? Explain.

Things To Do

1. Somebody said, "For every rule there are exceptions." Write one rule that you believe a person should follow. Describe a situation in which you feel it would be right for a person to break that rule.
2. Write a story in which you help a prisoner escape. Explain why the person was being held prisoner. Describe what you did to help him or her escape.

The Wayfarer

Stephen Crane

The wayfarer,
Perceiving the pathway to truth,
Was struck with astonishment.
It was thickly grown with weeds.
"Ha," he said,
"I see that none has passed here
In a long time."
Later he saw that each weed
Was a singular knife.
"Well," he mumbled at last,
"Doubtless there are other roads."

Code
of the Sea

Roger B. Goodman

In this story you will read about a "code" of the sea. The word "code" means a collection of rules for behavior. For example, a well-educated man in the 1800s was supposed to behave according to a "gentleman's code." Do you have a code of behavior? Read the story to find out what Captain Cyril's code was.

"Women and children first!"

That's part of one of the oldest codes of the sea.

"The captain goes down with his ship!"

That's another part.

The theory is that the captain is responsible for everything and everybody on board his ship. And if anything happens as a result of his carelessness, he is supposed to stay with his vessel. No matter what.

On a cold but calm January day, the schooner Laurel sailed out of Boston harbor. On board were Captain Earl Cyril, his wife Mary, their big, black Labrador retriever, and a crew of four. The little schooner had no radio on board. It had been left behind to be repaired.

As the Laurel sailed out into the Atlantic, the weather changed suddenly, as it can in the winter time. A fierce wind blew up. The waves grew up to 10 feet high. Captain Cryil, an old, experienced skipper, decided to turn back to port. But the pounding of the waves and the fury of the wind prevented this. Soon the schooner was wallowing in the water. The great waves began to pound her to pieces.

Captain Cyril gave the order to abandon ship. A launch was lowered into the water. Then the captain and his wife lowered a rowboat, got into it, and left the sinking schooner.

While the captain rowed away from the Laurel, he noticed that his dog was in the rowboat with him and his wife.

"How did the dog get into the boat, Mary?" roared the captain over the wind.

"One of the men put him in," she answered.

Then, as he rowed, the captain saw four of his crewmen swimming in the water. He steered his rowboat through the high waves so that they could grab onto it. He had great difficulty managing to keep the boat afloat.

"Captain," called out one of the men in the water, "get rid of that dog and let us get into the boat."

"No," answered the skipper. "You'll tip us all over."

The water was freezing. The waves were still high, but the sea was calming down a bit.

Again the men in the water begged for help. "Let one of us in at a time," said one. "We'll rotate in and out of the water. That way we can make it."

The captain picked up an oar. "I'll brain the first man that tries to climb aboard," he bellowed.

Gradually the men in the water became silent. Then, as the hours dragged by, their heads fell forward into the water. Their frozen hands slipped from the edge of the boat. Three of them slid down into the chill waters of the Atlantic.

Early the next morning, when the cold light of dawn crept over the water, a passing freighter spotted the drifting lifeboat. On board were the captain, his wife, the dog, and one crewman who had managed to climb on board during the night.

"I'll see you hang for this, Captain," the sailor said when they were all resting in the freighter's cabin. "You could have saved those men. But you chose to save your dog!"

"I did everything I could," replied Captain Cyril.

"You could have chucked that dog into the ocean. You saved him instead of your men!" The sailor was almost crying in his rage.

"I couldn't do that. The boat would have tipped over. We'd all be dead."

"You should be! You should be!" screamed the sailor. "You should have gone down with them. I hope you burn in hell for it!"

Then the sailor broke down and began to sob.

The big, black furry dog lay at his master's feet. He looked up into Captain Cyril's face. Then he wagged his tail slowly, as though to thank the captain for saving his life.

Captain Cyril gently stroked the dog's huge head. And he shook his own head sadly.

Building Your Vocabulary

1. The captain disregarded the *code* of the sea when he failed to help the crew. A *code* (p. 63) is a (A) collection of rules (B) type of game (C) destination (D) problem
2. The captain's *theory* was that if he rescued the men, the lifeboat might tip over. A *theory* (p. 63) is a (A) fact (B) belief (C) fear (D) religion
3. A court of law might decide that the captain was *responsible* for the sailors' deaths. To be *responsible* for (p. 63) means to be (A) a witness to (B) truthful about (C) sorry for (D) the cause of
4. The *schooner* set sail for Spain. A *schooner* (p. 64) is a kind of (A) animal (B) ship (C) plane (D) fish
5. The *Labrador retriever* stood on the deck and barked. A *Labrador retriever* (p. 63) is a kind of (A) machine (B) dog (C) boat (D) whistle
6. The people were *wallowing* helplessly in the water. *Wallowing* (p. 63) means (A) singing (B) freezing (C) floundering (D) perspiring
7. The sailors begged the captain not to *abandon* them. *Abandon* (p. 63) means to (A) kill (B) leave (C) beat (D) strip
8. The *launch* went through the waves with no difficulty. A *launch* (p. 63) is a kind of (A) oar (B) sail (C) boat (D) flag
9. The sailors decided to *rotate* the position of watchman. *Rotate* (p. 64) means to (A) take charge of (B) take turns at (C) help out with (D) work hard at
10. She *chucked* the rest of the bullets into her knapsack. *Chucked* (p. 65) means (A) cleaned (B) tossed (C) froze (D) cooked

Understanding the Story

Choosing Another Title

1. Which title tells most about the story?
(A) An Ocean Voyage (B) Ships at Sea (C) A Dog That Loved the Sea (D) A Captain's Choice

Finding Details

2. The name of the ship was
(A) Laura (B) Lucy (C) Laurel (D) Labrador
3. The ship could not call for help because
(A) the radio was broken (B) the radio had been washed overboard (C) there was no radio on board (D) no other ship was near
4. When the schooner sank,
(A) everybody got off (B) the dog was left behind (C) the captain stayed behind (D) the crew members stayed aboard
5. The drifting lifeboat was finally seen by someone
(A) in a helicopter (B) in a passenger plane (C) in a passing freighter (D) on shore
6. The captain was accused of
(A) saving his wife instead of the sailors (B) leaving his sinking ship (C) saving his dog instead of his men (D) being crazy
7. Captain Cyril said that the reason for his final decision was that
(A) he didn't know any men were in the water
(B) the men might have tipped over the lifeboat
(C) he valued the dog more than the men
(D) he was not in his right mind
8. How many people were saved after the ship sank?
(A) Two (B) Three (C) Four (D) Five

Using Your Reason

9. This story best illustrates the
    (A) dangers of a winter storm (B) love of a dog for
    his master (C) life of a sailor (D) way one person
    saved himself at the expense of others
10. The sailor who was saved felt
    (A) angry and wanted revenge (B) sad and wanted
    comfort (C) scared and wanted freedom
    (D) depressed and wanted peace

You Be the Judge

1. The idea of saving "women and children first" in
    case of a disaster is almost universal. Do you think
    it makes sense? Why?
2. Do you think the captain should be punished? If
    so, what punishment do you think would be
    appropriate?

3. We frequently read of people who risk—and sometimes lose—their lives to save pets from fires or floods. Would you take risks for a pet cat or dog? If so, what risks would you take?

Things To Do

1. Make a list of the *objects* you own. Which objects are most important to you? Which ones would you risk your own safety to save? What is important to you about these objects?
2. Sometimes during war or other great emergencies, enormous risks are taken to preserve precious works of art—paintings, sculpture, and so on. Would you risk your safety for a work of art? Why?
3. Speak to members of your local Fire Department unit. Ask them for true stories of incidents in which firefighters or civilians have rescued people, pets, or other valuables at great risk to themselves.

A Boy, a Rope,
and a Truth

Roger B. Goodman

Winning isn't everything, it's just the only thing.

—Vince Lombardi

Do you agree with this quote? See if your opinion changes after reading this story.

Johnny Romero had a dream. Well, really, he had more than one dream. For example, he dreamed that someday he would be an accountant. He always loved math, and he was good at it. He knew that he would have to work very hard at school. He also knew that he would probably have to go to college. But that was a long-range dream. For Johnny was in junior high school. Johnny Romero had a short-range dream too.

He wanted to become the rope-climbing champion of the Valley's schools. Johnny was short. And he was very fast. But he was too small to play basketball. Once when he tried out for the team, some of the bigger boys tried to use *him* for a basketball! And when he tried out for short-stop on the school baseball team, he was not as fast as Angel Torres. So, Angel, who was Johnny's best friend, got the position.

But Johnny was very good on the ropes. He could scramble up the line like a cat. His hands and arms were very strong. And because he was light, he could really fly up to the top. But his trouble was that, as fast as Johnny was, Angel was just a little faster.

One day, after he had lost to Angel again in a rope-climbing race, Johnny felt very unhappy.

71

"Ah, c'mon," said Angel to his friend. "Don't be so sad. It's not that important, you know. It's only a game."

"Yeah, yeah, I know," mumbled Johnny. "But once, just once I'd like to come in first. I'd like to be best in something."

"Well," answered Angel, "you're my best friend. Maybe that should mean something."

Johnny smiled at his friend. "Of course it means something. It means a lot. But I'd still like to beat you in climbing."

Both boys felt very good to know that they were really good friends. Because they were friends, they didn't mind racing against each other. That was part of their friendship.

And Johnny practiced. Almost every day, after school, he would go into the gym. The gym teacher, Mr. Elam, would be there. Mr. Elam liked Johnny very much. And he admired the way Johnny kept trying. He coached the boy. He taught him how to leap at the rope when the signal was given. And he cheered him on. Day after day the two of them would work. Mr. Elam would shout, "Go!"

Johnny would leap at the rope. He would pull himself up to the top. The rope was 15 feet high. Then Johnny would touch the ceiling just over the top of the rope. And he would slide down.

The school record for the rope climb was 2.1 seconds. It had been made three years before. Nobody had come close to breaking it. That is until Johnny Romero had come to the school. He had tied the record several times. And so had Angel Torres. But neither of them could break the record.

Finally, after two years of hard and steady training, Johnny was ready to try again. It was on a fine day at the end of the term. The whole gym class was there. Everybody knew that there would be a close race between Johnny and Angel. Each boy would have three tries at the record.

There was excitement as the two boys got ready for the contest. Angel was a little bigger than Johnny. He was a little heavier, too. And he was very popular with his fellow students.

"Let's go, Angel!" they chanted.

Angel smiled and waved to them. He rubbed his hands together. He crouched a little.

"Go!" shouted Mr. Elam.

Angel leaped and sped up the rope. He was up and down almost before anyone could blink an eye. "2.2 seconds!" called out the coach. The class broke into cheers. Johnny patted Angel on the back.

Then Johnny crouched for his start.

"Go!" shouted Mr. Elam.

Johnny scrambled up the rope like lightning. He slapped the top. Then he slid down.

"Great!" shouted the coach. "That was 2.1 seconds. You tied the record!"

Angel ran over. He hugged Johnny. "You'll do it now, Johnny," he said. "I know you can do it!"

73

Now it was Angel's turn again. Once more he was up and down in a flash. His second time also tied the record. But it seemed that he was getting tired.

Now it was Johnny's second attempt. The gym was very quiet.

"Go!" Mr. Elam shouted.

Up went Johnny like a flash. When he slid down, the coach gave a great shout. "Two seconds! Two seconds, Johnny! You broke the record!"

Angel ran over and grabbed Johnny. He lifted him right off his feet. Everybody was shouting and cheering. But Johnny looked very glum. He shook his head. His eyes were very sad. He walked over to Mr. Elam.

"What's the matter, Johnny?" asked Mr. Elam. "Next time you'll do even better."

"I didn't touch the top, coach." Johnny's voice was a whisper. "I didn't really touch."

Nobody but Johnny could tell that he had not put his hand on the ceiling. From the ground it looked as though he had done so. But he shook his head. "I didn't do it," he said again.

The coach turned to the class. Everyone was very quiet. "I want to tell you something," said Mr. Elam. And his voice was very serious. "Johnny did not set the record in the rope climb. But I think he did something even more important. He told the truth. And he told it even when he knew it could hurt him. And that's something any real champ would be proud of." And the coach patted Johnny on the shoulder.

Now it was Angel's turn. But this time he didn't even come close to the record. He was too tired. He shook his head sadly. Then it was Johnny's turn again.

It was even quieter than before in the gym. All eyes were on Johnny. Everyone seemed to stop breathing. It was clear that the whole class was hoping that Johnny would succeed. Everybody wanted him to break the record.

"Go!" shouted Mr. Elam.

Johnny was up and down the rope before anybody could breathe. He looked at the coach.

"You did it! You did it, Johnny! 1.9 seconds. You broke the record!" The coach was almost screaming.

A roar broke from the crowd. Everybody was jumping up and down and shouting. Angel and Johnny were jumping and pounding each other. It seemed as though the crowd would never settle down. But when they did, Mr. Elam raised his arms.

"OK! OK!" he yelled. "We've got a new champ. The whole Valley has a new champ. I don't think anyone is going to break this record for a long time. But I know one thing. Nobody will ever break Johnny's other record." Mr. Elam paused to look over at Johnny. "Nobody will break the record of telling the truth the way Johnny did. Even when he was the only person to know. And even when he knew how much it would hurt. That's a real championship record!"

Building Your Vocabulary

1. An *accountant* keeps records of the money spent and received by a business or a person. An *accountant* (p. 71) must be good in math because he deals with (A) people (B) numbers (C) businesses (D) customers
2. The cat *crouched* on the floor, then jumped up on the table. *Crouched* (p. 73) means kept the body (A) low (B) rigid (C) straight (D) stiff
3. As soon as the coach gave the signal, Johnny leaped and *scrambled* up the rope. *Scrambled* (p. 73) means (A) ran fast (B) moved swiftly (C) walked slowly (D) fell
4. *In a flash* the girl ran down the street to catch the bus. *In a flash* (p. 74) means (A) seriously (B) very quickly (C) angrily (D) gracefully
5. When he knew he had lost, Bruce smiled bravely but felt very *glum*. *Glum* (p. 74) means (A) happy (B) calm (C) frightened (D) sad

Understanding the Story

Choosing Another Title

1. Which title tells most about the story? (A) The Best Way To Climb (B) The Boy Who Told the Truth (C) High School Sports (D) The Gym Teacher

Finding Details

2. Johnny Romero wanted eventually to become

(A) a baseball star (B) a gym teacher (C) a banker
(D) an accountant
3. Johnny was excellent in
(A) math (B) all sports (C) history (D) football
4. Johnny lost the position of shortstop to
(A) a teacher (B) a new student (C) his best friend
(D) an eighth grader
5. Johnny did not get on the basketball team
because he was
(A) a poor shot (B) too slow (C) short (D) heavy
6. Angel Torres was happy that Johnny was
(A) his friend (B) smaller than he (C) one grade
behind him in school (D) going to a different
school
7. Where did the final contest take place?
(A) In another school (B) In the stadium
(C) Outdoors (D) In the school gym
8. How many tries did each person have to climb
the rope?
(A) One (B) Two (C) Three (D) Four

Using Your Reason

9. According to the story, telling the truth is a good
thing (A) once in a while (B) even if it hurts (C) in
order to make friends (D) if you have nothing to
lose
10. When Johnny broke the record, Angel was
(A) excited (B) angry (C) jealous (D) upset

You Be the Judge

1. Is it possible to go through life happily without
being "best in something"? Explain.

2. Why did Johnny admit he didn't "touch the top" even though nobody noticed it? What would you have done? Why?
3. How believable was it for Angel, who lost, to congratulate Johnny, who won? Explain.
4. Suppose the winner of the rope-climbing contest received a big money prize. Would the characters in this story behave differently? Why?

Things To Do

Write a paragraph beginning with any one of the following sentences:

A. The reason honesty is the best policy is that . . .
B. The difference between a winner and a loser is that a winner . . .
C. The way to be a winner is to . . .
D. The reason some people are never happy is that they . . .
E. I would rather lose than win, if winning meant . . .

A Timely Warning

Anonymous

If your nose is close to the grindstone rough,
And you hold it down there long enough,
In time you'll say there's no such thing
As brooks that babble and birds that sing.
These three will all your world compose:
Just You, the Stone, and your own old Nose.

The Servant

S. T. Semyonov

Have you ever meant to do something helpful and have everything turn out wrong? We all have to live with the results or consequences of our actions. But sometimes we don't realize what the consequences are going to be —as in this story.

For three months Gerasim had been seeking a job. Vainly he had wandered back and forth through the streets of Moscow. He was hungry. He was cold. He was desperate.

One day, by a stroke of luck, he met a friend from his home village. This friend, Yegor by name, was coachman to a wealthy merchant who lived at the far end of Moscow.

"What luck to meet you, Yegor," said Gerasim.

"What are you doing in Moscow?" returned Yegor. "How are things going for you?"

"Very badly," answered Gerasim. "I quit my last job, and I've been without work for weeks."

"Didn't you try to get your old job back?"

"Yes, I did. But the boss wouldn't take me back."

"Hmph," grunted Yegor coldly. "That's the way it is with you young fellows. Get a job and leave. And then expect someone to kick someone else out of a job just to take you back."

"That's true," agreed Gerasim. "But then, not everybody works as well and faithfully as you do, Yegor. That's why you've held your job for so long. It's hard to find men like you."

81

The Servant

Yegor grunted again, but Gerasim could see that his flattery had begun to work.

"Well," grumbled Yegor, "times are hard. I guess a man ought to help a fellow villager when he can. Maybe I can do something for you."

"You mean your master might have a place for me?" To Gerasim this seemed too good to be true.

"Well, maybe. Of course, if I speak to him it will be all right. He usually does what I say," boasted Yegor. "Right now he has a couple of servants. But they're old and lazy. I'll tell him he can get a young, strong servant and save money at the same time. He always likes the idea of saving money."

So Yegor and Gerasim walked across the city to the home of Yegor's employer. It was a great and impressive house. There was a huge courtyard outside. There were many stables and buildings where the servants lived. Yegor told Gerasim to wait outside.

Several minutes later Yegor came out of the main house. He had a great smile on his face.

"It's all set, my friend. The master says he'll be glad to hire you. But," and here Yegor's face became stern, "make sure you work hard. If you cause any trouble—just the least little bit—out you go! And it won't make things any easier for me, either."

"Don't worry! Don't worry! I'll be the best servant you ever saw. When do I start?"

"You come back here tomorrow morning, and you'll start right away. And we'll even have a room for you. Where the old people are now. They're leaving tomorrow morning."

"The old people?" Gerasim seemed puzzled.

"I told you," snorted Yegor. "They've been here a long time. But they're too weak and lazy to work any more. Youth before age, you know. Now the job's yours. And the room. You're a very lucky young man."

82

Gerasim was amazed at his good luck. A job and a place to stay. A room of his own. He shook Yegor's hand. "I'll be here bright and early. Don't you worry."

Gerasim was eager to make a good impression. He returned to his new master's house even before it was daylight. As he was waiting in the chilly courtyard, he passed one of the servant's houses. The light was on inside. He heard the sound of weeping from within. Very quietly he sneaked up to the window and looked inside.

The room was tiny but very neat and clean. In the middle of the floor was a great sack into which clothes had been piled. Seated at the plain, wooden table were two elderly people. One was a gray haired, bent old man. The other was his equally gray haired and bent old wife. They were sobbing.

"Twenty years of work! Twenty years of my life," groaned the man.

"And now we're thrown out. Like a couple of old horses."

"Horses would be better off," wept his wife. "At least they're put out to graze and to live in peace. Where can we go? What can we do? We'll starve to death."

In silence, then, they both continued weeping. Gerasim slowly crept away from the window. His face was pale with shock and dismay. His eyes were almost filled with tears. This was something he had not really expected. At first it had seemed like some kind of a joke. As Yegor had said, "Youth before age." But there was something that bothered Gerasim. When he saw that old couple weeping in their bare little room, he almost saw his own parents in their poor hovel back in his home village.

How long he stood in the courtyard, Gerasim didn't really know. But all of a sudden he saw Yegor, bustling and cheery, running across towards him.

"Promptness! Promptness! That's what the master likes, Gerasim. I told him what a good worker you'd be. Come on now, I want you to meet him." And Yegor put a great, heavy arm around Gerasim's shoulders.

"I don't know," muttered Gerasim.

"What?" bellowed Yegor. "What do you mean, 'I don't know'? Is that your idea of a joke?"

"No," replied Gerasim. He shrugged Yegor's arm from his shoulder. "I just think I changed my mind. I want to thank you ever so much—I'll never be able to repay your kindness—but I think I'll look for a job somewhere else. On my own."

Yegor was red with rage. "What do you mean? I go out of my way to tell the master all sorts of stories about you —how good you are—and how loyal. I even have him sack two people who've been working for him for twenty years. And this is your thanks. What kind of nonsense is this?"

"It's no nonsense." Gerasim suddenly felt much stronger. "I'm truly sorry for all your troubles, Yegor. But I think I'll try for myself—somewhere else. Tell the master to give the two old people their job back."

With a curse Yegor spun on his heel and walked away. Gerasim looked after him for a moment. Then, with a grin on his face, he walked out of the courtyard. For the first time in many months he felt really young again. And he was happy and lighthearted as he strolled down towards the center of the city.

Building Your Vocabulary

1. Gerasim was unhappy because he had been looking *vainly* for work for weeks. *Vainly* (p. 81) means (A) easily (B) barely (C) stupidly (D) unsuccessfully
2. Not being able to find a job can make a person feel *desperate*. *Desperate* (p. 81) means (A) lonely (B) hopeless (C) lucky (D) serious
3. Gerasim saw that Yegor's reaction was negative when Yegor grunted *coldly*. *Coldly* (p. 81) means (A) gladly (B) quietly (C) unsympathetically (D) with a cough

4. People sometimes use *flattery* to get someone to do them favors. *Flattery* (p. 82) means (A) the truth (B) insincere praise (C) a joke (D) shaking hands

5. The house's great size, its white paint, and the beautiful gardens around it were *impressive*. *Impressive* (p. 82) means (A) awesome (B) sorrowful (C) happy (D) ugly

6. Yegor's face was cold and had a *stern* expression when he told Gerasim that he must work hard. *Stern* (p. 82) means (A) smiling (B) serious (C) questioning (D) mild

7. The *dismay* that Gerasim felt when he saw the sad old people showed that he was a kindly person. *Dismay* (p. 84) means (A) confusion (B) anger (C) happiness (D) eagerness

8. The poor people lived in a *hovel* made of stone and clay. A *hovel* (p. 84) is a (A) stable (B) shack (C) tent (D) garage

9. *Promptness* in getting to work pleases one's boss. *Promptness* (p. 84) means (A) tardiness (B) quickness (C) carelessness (D) slowness

10. Yegor's master cruelly *sacked* the two people who had worked for him for 20 years. *Sacked* (p. 85) means (A) gave a job to (B) fired (C) sent on an errand (D) rewarded

Understanding the Story

Choosing Another Title

1. Which title tells most about the story?
   (A) How To Find Work (B) Life on a Plantation
   (C) A Good Deed (D) The Lazy Person

Finding Details

2. Gerasim had been seeking work
   (A) for several years (B) for two weeks (C) all his
   life (D) for three months
3. The coachman who attempted to help Gerasim
   was named
   (A) Yegor (B) Ivan (C) Gregor (D) Slovin
4. Gerasim was out of work because he had
   (A) been fired (B) quit his job (C) stole some
   money (D) been in the army
5. In addition to a job Gerasim was offered
   (A) an increase in pay (B) his own coach
   (C) a room of his own (D) an assistant
6. Gerasim was so eager to make a good impression
   that he
   (A) waited all night in the courtyard (B) returned
   before daylight (C) bought a new cap (D) offered
   to work for less
7. The situation of the old people came to Gerasim's
   attention when he
   (A) heard them cursing him (B) saw them moving
   away (C) heard them weeping (D) was told about
   it by their friends
8. When Gerasim saw the old people, it made him
   think of
   (A) his own old age (B) the way time quickly
   passes (C) his own parents (D) the advantages of
   youth

Using Your Reason

9. The story shows that self-sacrifice is sometimes
   (A) stupid (B) unpopular (C) impossible
   (D) unbelievable

10. You can tell from the story that the master
believed he should
(A) take care of loyal servants (B) provide fair
wages for all the servants (C) obtain servants that
would be useful to him (D) provide old servants
with a fair living

You Be the Judge

1. "Heaven helps those who help themselves."
"What you do not want done to yourself, do not do
to others."

   These are two statements about the way persons
should conduct their lives. They point in opposite
directions. Gerasim could have followed either one.
Which one do you think better explains the way he
behaved? Why?
2. Suppose you had tried very hard to get a friend of
yours on a team. After having been accepted, your
friend decided not to join the team. What would
your reaction be? What reasons might justify your
friend's action in your mind?

Things To Do

1. Interview several older people you know who are
no longer working. Find out how many want to
work but cannot find jobs. What is their attitude
toward growing old? What is their attitude toward
working?
2. Some people lose their jobs because they are old.
Some people cannot get jobs because of their

advanced age. However, some employers say that older workers are reliable, efficient, and trustworthy. Write a paragraph beginning with one of the following sentences:
(A) If I were an employer, I would hire older workers because ... (B) If I were an employer, I would hire young workers because ...

Paul's Poppa

Roger B. Goodman

We learn much of our behavior by imitating others—usually older members of our family. In this story you will read how a father's good example affects his son.

Poppa! Poppa! Why did you do it?"

Paul Rodriguez leaned over his father. The tears were streaming down his face.

There was a crowd pushing and shoving all around him, but all Paul could see was his father. The man was lying on the dirty street, his hands bloody. He was holding them over the deep wound in his stomach. A dirty newspaper was under his head. He looked up at his weeping son.

"Paul," he whispered. "Don't cry! I'll be all right. Take care of your mother."

Then he smiled a little smile. "I did it because I had to."

At this point the ambulance came up, its siren screeching. The medics ran through the crowd. They put Paul's father, José, on a stretcher and placed him gently into the ambulance. Then they sped away.

Paul stood up and wiped his eyes. A reporter came up to him with a microphone. The reporter was from a TV news program.

"Did you know that man?" he asked Paul.

"Yes," said Paul, trying not to cry. "He's my poppa."

"Can you tell us what happened?" asked the man.

"How did he get stabbed?"

Paul saw the microphone that the reporter was holding. He saw the TV camera pointed at him. A couple of days ago, he would have been really excited about being on TV. Now, though, it didn't make any difference.

"He got stabbed because he was minding somebody else's business." Paul sounded bitter. "He wasn't even on duty. He just retired, so he isn't even a cop anymore."

"So your father was a police officer!" Now the man sounded excited.

Paul was proud of his father.

"Well, what happened?"

The people were crowding around. At first Paul was angry. Where were they when his father needed them? They all could have helped. Then Paul figured that it would be important to tell the story.

"We were just going over to the pizza place to get a pizza for supper. Then my poppa saw something going on over at the grocery store. He saw some men beating the owner. They had dragged him out of the store. They were beating him with rocks and sticks. He was yelling for help, but nobody came. Everybody acted like nothing was happening." Here Paul looked out at the crowd standing around. Some of the men looked away. They seemed to be ashamed.

"When my poppa saw what was going on, he ran across the street," Paul continued. "He yelled for me to call the cops. I heard him yell, 'Police officer! Cut it out!' And he wasn't even a cop any more. Anyway, he began pulling them off the man. He knocked two of them down. The other two ran away. My poppa grabbed one. And then . . . and then . . ." Paul started to sob.

"What happened then, son?" said the TV reporter.

"One of those cowards pulled his knife. He stabbed my poppa in the belly. And he ran away, the dirty . . . If anything happens—if my poppa dies . . ." Paul started crying hard. And the man put his arm around Paul's shoulder.

"Your poppa will be all right. He must be tough. I guess he felt somebody had to help. And he thought he was the person to do it."

"That's what poppa always told me," said Paul. When nobody helps people, everybody gets hurt. It could be me or momma, poppa says, or my little sister Angelita. My poppa always told me that. That's why he was a cop."

Later on that night, Paul went to see his father in the hospital. José Rodriguez' stomach was covered with bandages. He was being given blood intravenously. When he saw his son, his eyes grew brighter. He smiled.

"Hi, Paul. How's momma and Angelita?"

"They're OK, poppa. How are you?"

"Fine, fine, Paul. I'm going to be OK. Hey, remember what you asked me?"

Paul looked puzzled. "No, I don't remember, poppa."

"You asked me why did I do it. Well, Paul, I did it because I'm a cop. Yeah, yeah, I know." José held up his hand when Paul tried to break in. "Yeah, I know I'm retired. But I'm a cop even without a uniform, Paul."

"How come, poppa. I don't get it. How come you're a cop even without a uniform, and nobody else is?"

"Ah, Paul. Everybody should be—a little bit. Just because everybody is a human being. When you hurt one human being, you hurt everybody."

"Yea, poppa. But what about momma and me and Angelita—our family? Don't you worry about us when you do things like that?"

"Paul!" José's eyes closed wearly. "It's just because I'm thinking of you and momma and Angelita that I do these things. And when lots of people start looking out for other people, then maybe everybody will be a lot safer."

José's voice trailed off. He closed his eyes. It was easy to see how tired he was.

Just then the nurse came by. She saw Paul sitting next to his father's bed, and she saw José sleeping.

She put her finger on her lips. "OK, now, son," she whispered, "let's just let him get some sleep now."

As they walked to the door of the room, the nurse took Paul's arm. "You've got a real good dad there, son. He'll be all right, don't you worry. And you should be proud of him, for what he did. There should be lots more like him."

Paul walked home slowly. He was thinking about what poppa had told him. Then he thought of what the nurse said. And he knew she was right—poppa was a good man, and Paul was proud of him.

Building Your Vocabulary

1. The ambulance rushed down the street with its
   siren *screeching. Screeching* (p. 91) means
   (A) moving fast (B) going away (C) making
   a shrill noise (D) stopping
2. They took a *stretcher* out of the back of the
   ambulance. A *stretcher* (p. 91) is used to
   (A) prepare paintings (B) carry sick or injured
   people (C) cover holes (D) move heavy objects
3. Paul was so *bitter* about the accident that he
   refused to talk or eat. *Bitter* (p. 92) means
   (A) calm and steady (B) distressed and resentful
   (C) loud and talkative (D) quiet and shy
4. Paul's father is *retired* and receives a well-earned
   pension. *Retired* (p. 92) means to be withdrawn
   from one's (A) occupation (B) house (C) friends
   (D) family
5. Because he could not eat, a needle was put in his
   arm through which he was fed *intravenously.*
   Intravenously (p. 93) means that something is put
   in the body by way of the (A) mouth (B) nose
   (C) veins (D) feet

Understanding the Story

Choosing Another Title

1. Which title tells most about the story?
   (A) The Work of a Police Officer (B) How To
   Become a Police Officer (C) Police Officer Without
   a Uniform (D) The Police and the Citizen

95

Paul's Poppa

Finding Details

2. Paul's father was named
   (A) Carlo (B) Ernesto (C) José (D) Fredric
3. As Paul's father ran across the street, he
   (A) told Paul to go home (B) called for help
   (C) drew his gun (D) told Paul to call the police
4. When this incident happened, Paul's father had
   just (A) joined the police force (B) entered the
   Police Academy (C) retired from the police force
   (D) joined the Marines
5. The members of Paul's family who lived at home
   included (A) a little brother (B) a grandmother
   (C) a little sister (D) an aunt
6. When the TV reporter first approached him, Paul
   (A) became excited (B) didn't really respond
   (C) became scared (D) began crying
7. As Paul spoke to the TV reporter, some people in
   the crowd
   (A) started laughing (B) seemed ashamed
   (C) yelled at him (D) cut the TV cable
8. Paul's father had been a
   (A) high school dropout (B) hero of the Viet Nam
   war (C) police officer (D) veteran of World War II

Using Your Reason

9. Paul's father did what he did because he
   (A) was a mean person (B) wanted to help
   someone (C) wanted his job back (D) had a gun
10 Which of the following sentences best illustrates
   the main idea of the story?
   (A) Might makes right.
   (B) People should help their neighbors.
   (C) People in glass houses shouldn't throw
   stones. (D) Lucky at love, unlucky at war.

You Be the Judge

1. A citizen fights with and defeats a mugger. Some people say citizens should call the police and let them take care of catching criminals. What do you think? Explain.
2. At one time in the United States there were groups of citizens called "vigilantes." These vigilantes would go about punishing people they thought were criminals. Sometimes they would kill people they thought were wrongdoers.

    Today in the United States it is illegal for people to take the law into their own hands. It is the job of a police officer to arrest people. Why do you think vigilantes are illegal? Do you think it is a good idea for people to take the law into their own hands? Explain.
3. There is sometimes a "conflict of loyalties" between social interests and personal interests. For instance, do you think it is right for the parents of young children to risk their lives to help a stranger as Paul's father did? Or do parents have a responsibility to keep themselves safe and alive? Explain.

Things To Do

1. Discuss with a police officer how a citizen can help the police. Find out the police officer's attitude toward citizens that try to stop a crime themselves.
2. Think of someone or something you are loyal to (school, friends, government, family, and so on). Think of a situation in which you would want to, or would feel that you should, do something that was disloyal. How would you resolve the conflict? Write a paragraph telling about it.

To Lie or
Not To Lie

Carla Fine

This story is about a young woman working in an office. Her supervisor urges her to "remember you're a professional." After reading the story, tell what you think it means to be "a professional."

This was Kathy Allen's big break. After six months in the typing pool at Patterson Publishers, she was now private secretary to Bill Duncan, Senior Editor.

Kathy was excited. She was also scared.

"What happens if I make mistakes?" she asked Ann Wescott, her supervisor.

"Look, Kathy," Ann answered, "you're a good secretary. That's why Bill asked for you. But you're not perfect —nobody is. Just remember you're a professional. You've got experience. If you make mistakes, learn from them. Take pride in yourself, and do the best job you can."

When Kathy Allen reported to Bill Duncan at nine o'clock sharp the next morning, he barely looked at her. "Here you are, Kathy," he said, handing her a huge bunch of letters. "Get these typed up as soon as you can. I hope you know how to spell."

The morning raced past. Kathy typed madly. Most of the letters she received were messy and needed correcting. Between typing and answering the telephone, Kathy's day sped past. She didn't even remember whether or not she had taken time out to have lunch. At the end of the day there was a good pile of letters waiting for Bill's signature. As he looked them over to sign them, he grunted every once in a while. Kathy figured out that meant everything was all right.

As time went by, Kathy began to enjoy being so busy. She knew her typing was excellent. Bill seemed pleased with her work. But there were a few things that began to bother her, like the time one of the other editors came to see Bill. Kathy knew that Bill was in his office. He had told her he would be there. But he also said, "Look, Kathy, I don't want to be disturbed. Tell everyone who calls or who drops by that I'm not in."

So Kathy told this editor, "I'm very sorry, but Bill is not in his office. Shall I have him call you back?"

The woman looked at Kathy in a strange and unfriendly way. She seemed to know the truth. But she didn't say anything. She just shrugged and walked away.

Kathy felt uncomfortable because she didn't like the idea of lying. It's true, these weren't "big" lies. But they were lies, and Kathy just didn't like the idea.

When Kathy spoke to Ann Wescott about her feelings, the supervisor simply laughed. "It's something you have to get used to, dear. It's lying, but it's not lying—if you know what I mean. Anyway, that's the way it's done in business. Don't worry too much about it."

But it did bother Kathy. And things piled up.

One day Kathy got a note from Henry Curtis, the President of Patterson Publishers. It announced an important meeting for all the senior editors. Kathy went in to Bill and handed him the note.

"Ah, these meetings," laughed Bill. "What a waste of time. Everybody just sits and gabs for hours. And nothing gets done."

He crumpled up the note and threw it into his wastepaper basket.

Early the next week, Henry Curtis dropped into the office personally. He smiled at Kathy as she announced him to her boss. He went into Bill's room.

When he came out a few minutes later, he seemed very angry. He barely looked at Kathy, and he did not return her smile. Then Bill came out.

"Listen, Kathy. I've got to talk to you. Come inside."

When Kathy got inside his office, Bill said, "Sit down." He smiled a little bit. "Listen, Kathy. I think I've been a pretty good boss to work for. Don't you agree?"

Kathy felt a tingle of fear. But she smiled. "Why, yes, Mr. Duncan. I'm very happy here."

"Good." he said. "Because I just did something I'm not proud of. Henry Curtis asked me why I had not been at that executive meeting last week. And I told him—I guess you could say I lied a little bit—I told him I had not received the notice."

"But, Mr. Duncan. I gave you that memo as soon as I got it. You . . ."

"I know. I know, Kathy. I threw it away myself. But I told Henry that you had never given it to me. I guess I was protecting myself. So I had to put the blame on you. I hope you understand."

Kathy was too stunned to say anything. She went back to her desk and just sat there. It all seemed so unfair. She was doing her job. She was even lying to protect her boss. And now he made her seem to be not only a liar but a poor

worker. She remembered what Ann Wescott had told her
—"Take pride in your work and do the best job you can."
She burst into tears.

Things were not exciting or enjoyable after that. Kathy
was still very efficient, but she did not feel happy. And
Bill had little to say to her. He was pleasant. He was even
kind. But he did not seem friendly or warm.

As Kathy grew more and more experienced on the job,
her responsibilities grew. It almost seemed as though she
were running the office. She made Bill's appointments.
She arranged his schedule so he could function most effi-
ciently. And she was an efficient and reliable secretary.
Most of the unpleasantness began to ease away.

Until the incident of the expense account. It was the
last Friday in March and Kathy was in a good mood. She
was looking forward to the weekend and to her vacation
which would be coming soon. Right now she was going
over Bill's expense account. He would write out a list of
his expenses for the month. Then Kathy would copy it on
the correct form so that the company would repay Bill.

She was copying Bill's pencilled list onto the form when
she noticed it: "March 17—luncheon for four—$75.00."

"That's impossible," Kathy thought. She remembered
that date clearly because it was St. Patrick's Day. Bill had
had an appointment with an author. But the luncheon
had been cancelled. Instead Bill had joined Kathy in
watching the Parade. And they had had lunch together.
A couple of hot dogs and soda.

Kathy went into Bill's office. "I think you made a mistake on this list," she said. "You wrote that you had lunch
with an author on St. Patrick's Day. But that lunch was
cancelled, don't you remember? You and I had a couple
of hot dogs at the Parade."

"Of course I remember, Kathy," smiled Bill. "It was a
lovely day."

102

3/9	Luncheon	$42.00
3/10	Luncheon for two	$75.00
3/14	Luncheon for two	$12.67
3/17	Luncheon for four	$34.00
	Reimbursement for Supplies	

"But you put down a $75.00 expense. I don't understand." Kathy was puzzled.

Bill laughed. "Oh, Kathy! It's time you knew that everyone does that in this business. You know—pad the expense account a little. This is a big company, Kathy. That $75.00 is like a drop in a bucket."

"But it's really cheating," said Kathy. "It's almost like stealing."

Bill stopped smiling. "Look, Kathy. I really don't have to be lectured by my secretary. Just fill out the form as I've indicated. I don't think there's anything more to talk about."

Kathy started walking out of the office. But she couldn't hold back any longer. She turned. "I'm sorry, Bill. I just don't think that what you're doing is right. I just can't fill out that form for you. And then put my initials on it."

Bill was silent for a minute. Then he spoke. "Look, Kathy. You've been the best secretary I've ever had. I was just going to put you in for a raise. I have the papers on my desk right now. But you'll have to learn not to see some things that go on around here. Or not to say anything if you do see them. That's the way it's got to be. There's no sense in being like a child—so idealistic. Or I guess you'll just have to go somewhere else. And I'd be truly sorry about that."

Kathy went out slowly. She sat down at her desk. Was

To Lie or Not to Lie

Bill trying to bribe her with that raise? If she stayed on, wouldn't it be as though she went along with all the lying and cheating? And wouldn't she become a part of it?

On the other hand, it wasn't really her problem. If anything ever happened, it would be Bill who had to come up with the answers. She just worked there.

And yet she had to live with herself and her own way of thinking and feeling. She had to take pride in her job.

She reached into the drawers of her desk and took out her purse. She took her hat and coat. Very slowly she went back to Bill's door. Softly she knocked. When Bill answered, she went in. He seemed surprised to see her carrying her things.

"What's the matter, Kathy?"

Kathy spoke softly, almost sadly. But she was quite firm. "Bill, I'm very sorry about this. I love this job, and I like working for you. But I guess I am still something of a child—I am still a little idealistic. And I just can't live a lie. So I'll have to look somewhere else to work. Goodby, Bill."

And before her astonished boss could say a word, Kathy turned and walked out.

Building Your Vocabulary

1. To save gasoline in driving to work, I joined a car *pool* with three of my friends. A *pool* (p. 99) is a (A) type of race (B) group that shares something (C) sale (D) family
2. Before boarding the plane for Los Angeles, Louis felt a *tingle* of fear. A *tingle* (p. 101) is a feeling that is (A) dull (B) prickly (C) soothing (D) short
3. Some people *pad* their expense accounts so they will be paid more than is due them. To *pad*

expenses (p. 103) means to (A) write them down
(B) exaggerate them (C) discuss them
(D) forget them
4. She said that it was *idealistic* to imagine that all
countries could live in peace. *Idealistic* (p. 103)
means (A) unusual (B) overoptimistic
(C) understandable (D) uncalled for
5. When the huge dog walked into the classroom the
teacher was *astonished* and then amused.
Astonished (p. 104) means (A) amazed
(B) frightened (C) impatient (D) happy

Understanding the Story

Choosing Another Title

1. Which title tells most about the story?
(A) The Secretary Gets a Raise (B) The Secretary
Wins Approval (C) The Perfect Secretary
(D) The Secretary's Problem

Finding Details

2. Kathy could tell when Bill was satisfied because
he (A) sent her flowers (B) grunted
(C) wrote her a note (D) stopped yelling at her
3. The first time Kathy knew that she was
uncomfortable with her job was when her boss
(A) criticized her spelling (B) was late to work
(C) asked her to lie (D) took her to dinner
4. Bill Duncan was a man who
(A) encouraged frequent meetings (B) liked to

make speeches (C) tried to avoid meetings
(D) went to meetings instead of writing letters

5. Henry Curtis gave Kathy Allen an angry look
because he thought she had
(A) lied (B) misplaced a memo (C) lost money for
the company (D) typed a letter poorly

6. As Kathy Allen became more experienced it
seemed to her that she was
(A) making more mistakes (B) working less and
less (C) running the office (D) getting tired

7. Bill Duncan argued that "padding the expense
account" was NOT cheating because the company
(A) owed him the money (B) could afford the
money (C) would never find out (D) also cheats

8. Kathy finally quit working for Bill when he asked
her to
(A) write up a false expense form (B) stay after
work (C) spend company money (D) lie to Ann
Wescott

Using Your Reason

9. Kathy Allen can best be described as
(A) mean (B) sensitive (C) lazy (D) carefree

10. Ann Wescott's attitude about lying was that
Kathy should
(A) go along with the boss's lies (B) lie only to
customers (C) never tell lies (D) lie only when
absolutely necessary

You Be the Judge

1. Kathy Allen had worked hard to reach her present
position. Should she have quit for the reason she
did? Explain.

2. Instead of quitting, Kathy Allen could have told the president of the company about Bill Duncan's cheating. What do you think would have happened if she had done that?
3. If you were in Kathy's place, what would you have done? Why?
4. If you had a choice between a very well-paid job in a big business where you would be expected to lie once in a while and a less well-paid job in an organization where you would not be expected to lie, which would you choose? Why?

Things To Do

1. Number these events in the order in which they happened in the story.
   Bill Duncan explains to Kathy Allen why Henry Curtis is angry.
   Bill asks Kathy to write up a false expense account.
   Kathy tells the editor that Bill is not in the office.
   Bill offers Kathy a raise.
   Henry Curtis barely looks at Kathy Allen and does not return her smile.
2. Rewrite the ending of the story. Show another way Kathy could have behaved. Tell what happens to her.
3. Pretend that you are a friend of Kathy's. Having just quit her job, she goes to the coffee shop downstairs where she meets you. Write a paragraph telling what the two of you might say.

Courage
Is Contagious

Roger B. Goodman
and Charles G. Spiegler

From the 12th century, Great Britain has exercised some control over Ireland. Complete control came in 1800 when the Act of Union broke up the Irish Parliament and transferred all legislative power to London.

Many Irish opposed British control. Resistance groups formed to oppose Great Britain. After much fighting, the present state of the Republic of Ireland was established in 1922. However, Northern Ireland (Ulster) did not join the Republic of Ireland. It had close economic and social ties to Great Britain. Many people in Ulster were Protestant. They were happy being part of Great Britain, a Protestant country.

A large minority of people in Ulster are Roman Catholic. Some want to be part of the Republic of Ireland. In 1968–1969 large demonstrations were held by Roman Catholics who said they were discriminated against by the Protestant government. British troops were called in to keep the peace. There was no settlement. The struggle continued with bombings and shootings. In more than a decade of conflict, over 1,700 persons have been killed.

What is it like for a family to live surrounded by violence? This story shows the bitter hatreds that can exist and the power that exists to overcome these hatreds.

It was an April morning in Belfast, Northern Ireland. Jackie McGowan had just let his wife and three children off in front of the supermarket. Then he went around back to park. When he heard the bomb, he raced around to the front. People were screaming and running in all directions. Smoke and flames were shooting out of the market. Jackie fought to get through the crowd.

"My family! My wife and kids!" he screamed.

The police and firefighters held him back. When the fire and smoke had died down, the men went into the ruins. Twisted and torn and horribly burned lay the bodies of Mrs. McGowan and her two older children. Baby Jackie, six weeks of age, curled in his dead mother's arms. In the midst of the rubble, the baby almost seemed asleep. His little face was calm and restful. His tiny lips curled in a baby smile.

Jackie McGowan gave a loud, wrenching scream when he saw his family. Then, fortunately, he collapsed.

That bomb was only the first of four. Altogether that week 12 people were killed—eight Catholics and four Protestants—among them six young children.

For generations, now, the bitter struggle between Catholics and Protestants has been spreading death and destruction throughout Northern Ireland. Children, young men and women, and older folk have been bombing, machine-gunning, and hurling rocks at each other. They have also been assaulting the British troops who are stationed in Ireland. It has been, up to now, a problem that seemed to have no solution.

Jackie McGowan went to stay with his sister-in-law, Annie Dolan. She and her husband Frank lived with their two children not far from the McGowans. Tenderly and lovingly she cared for Jackie, trying to calm and soothe his pain and his anger. But inwardly she too was furious. All the killing! All the wee ones and men and women blown to bits. And for what? She could never answer that question. Nor could her husband, Frank; nor Jackie.

Up to now the Dolans had been very lucky. Frank's job was all the way on the other side of town. He had to drive through the most dangerous areas to get there. But he had never even been close to injury. Annie prayed constantly for him and for her children. And she prayed for all Ireland with its bloody days and nights.

110

One day, about a month or two after these tragic events, Annie Dolan decided to go downtown to do some shopping. The sky above Belfast was clear and sharp blue. There was a touch of warmth in the air. The town was quiet. The streets were still empty. The stores and cafes were shut. Occasionally someone could be seen scuttling along to early Mass. But it was pleasantly quiet.

As the morning wore on, people came out of their homes. The shutters on the shops were taken down. Delivery vans began going through the streets, and a few schoolboys, whistling cheerfully, raced towards their classes.

Annie kissed her two boys goodbye. She told Jennie, the neighbor's daughter, to keep an eye on them and to give them lunch at noon. Then feeling cheerful and happy for the first time in a long while, she began walking toward the shopping center. Here and there among the busy shops and buses were dark, gaping holes. Annie crossed herself when she passed them and breathed a prayer. For those were the wrecked shops where the bombs had gone off. They were scarred with smoke and the smell of death.

Downtown, in the heart of the shopping district, everything was bustling and bright. People were scurrying in and out of shops. They stopped to gossip with their friends. Kids laughed and cried and chased each other all over the sidewalks. It seemed as though all the trouble and pain were miles and years away. Even those who had suffered terrible losses of family and friends seemed to feel lighter in heart. Everything seemed to indicate that there was hope for the suffering people. Of course, there had been this feeling before. This time, however, it seemed real.

Annie picked up a few toys for her children. And luckily, she managed to find, on sale, a pretty frock she had been wanting to buy for some time. So, all in all, when she got ready to return to her house, she was in a fine, happy frame of mind. As she began walking back, she passed through the large square in front of the church. As always, she went in. She always lit a candle for the souls of those who had been brutally killed in the bombings. Actually, it made no difference to her whether they were Catholic or Protestant. "A wee dead baby is just a wee dead baby," she always said. "I think it makes God just as sad whether it's Catholic or Protestant. Or anything at all." And she would breathe a prayer of thanks for the safety of her own family. She would pray that soon all these troubles would be over. "If only there were something I could do more than just to pray," she whispered to herself.

As she emerged from the darkness of the church into the sunlit street, she noticed a British soldier walking along. He had his rifle slung across his back, and he was walking with his hand resting gently on the shoulders of a little boy. The little fellow was riding his bike, wobbling a bit, and talking cheerfully to his soldier friend. It was a pleasant and friendly scene.

112

Suddenly, without the slightest warning, there was the blazing crackle of machine-gun fire. It came from the porch of the church. The little boy gave a shriek and fell over the handlebars of his bike. The soldier, quick as a flash, threw himself on the little boy, shielding the child with his body. The machine gun clattered again. This time the soldier's body shook violently. It was as though a giant hand was ripping him to pieces. It was all over in a few seconds. The bright day was shattered. In the middle of the square, twisting in a pool of blood, lay the bodies of the soldier and the little boy. People screamed, and the shoppers scattered to shelter.

Annie, without even knowing what she was doing, ran out into the square. She knew, as a good Catholic, that it was one's duty to whisper the Act of Contrition to a dying man. And she felt that it might be right to do it for any person—Catholic or Protestant, in uniform or not. But she was so shaken by the suddenness of the event that she forgot the words of the prayer. All she could keep repeating was, "You know what I mean, God. You know what I mean."

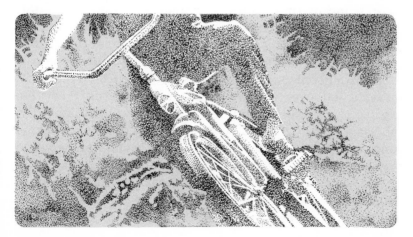

113

She was so involved in what she was doing and so stunned by the sight before her, that she did not know what was going on around her until the first stone struck her in the head. She looked up. Standing in a circle around her, screaming with rage and fury, was a crowd of women.

"Good for the British swine," they screamed. "Go on and pray, soldier lover. You'll need it!"

They spat at Annie and continued throwing rocks.

Annie Dolan remained on her knees praying and trying to shield the bodies of the two murdered human beings. She wept with anger and frustration. But she remained there, praying.

The stones rained harder and harder on Annie's head and body. She bent closer to the little boy's body. Then, suddenly, almost unaware of what she was doing, Annie stood up. She grasped the broken, bleeding little body in her arms. The women stopped shouting. Annie, with the blood and tears streaming down her own face, began walking. The women drew back. They made a lane in front of her.

As she walked past the church, Annie saw two young men standing there leaning against the church and chatting. One of them moved towards her with a grin on his face. She gave him a look of such hate and contempt that he stopped in his tracks. She didn't know where she was walking. People stared at her as she went by. A terrible silence fell over the whole town. Then Annie became aware of a sound behind her. Looking over her shoulder, she saw a great crowd of women—many of them the same ones who had been stoning her—walking behind her. And women from the sidewalks were joining in.

She was passing the Communications Building now. Suddenly a man came running out of the building. He had a microphone in his hand. Right behind him was another man with a camera. The man with the mike stopped in front of Annie.

"What's this all about, Missus?" he said. "Whose little one is this?"

Like a flash it dawned on Annie what she must do. "I don't know whose little one this is," she said. Her voice was quite calm and clear. "But he's my little son. And Belfast's. And Ireland's. And we'll go on slaughtering him like we did our Saviour until some of us decide to put a stop to it."

She turned around and held the little boy's body towards the great crowd of women. "How many more of our little ones will you be sacrificing, then? Is this what we bear 'em for, to be blown to bits in the marketplace? If you're with me, women, let 'em hear it on the telly. And let's let 'em hear it all 'round the world."

The woman gave a great shout that ended with a universal sob. A police officer took the little boy from Annie's shaking arms. And she, now tired and quivering all over, knew what she must do.

From this incident, a great organization for peace was formed in Northern Ireland. By getting hundreds and then thousands of women to sign petitions and to begin to speak out against the terror, Annie started a people's peace movement. It spread through all of Ireland, into England, and even reached the United States. As Annie has said, "Fear is contagious, but also courage is contagious."

Building Your Vocabulary

1. After the bomb had hit the building, the police began digging through the *rubble. Rubble* (p. 110)

means (A) ground (B) cellar (C) broken pieces (D) sidewalk

2.   When Larry's mother saw his black eye and bleeding face, she gave a *wrenching* cry. *Wrenching* (p. 110) means (A) laughing (B) tearful (C) silent (D) strained and twisted

3.   The *tragic* events of the riots in Northern Ireland will not soon be forgotten. *Tragic* (p. 111) means (A) recent (B) delightful (C) making people work (D) especially unfortunate

4.   Dodging cars and buses, the old man was *scuttling* across the street. *Scuttling* (p. 111) means (A) sinking (B) scurrying (C) riding (D) sliding

5.   The long, cold winter left many *gaping* holes in the streets. *Gaping* (p. 111) means (A) tiny (B) wide open (C) long and narrow (D) circular

6.   A *bustling,* noisy crowd rushed in for the coat sale. *Bustling* (p. 112) means (A) merry (B) busily hurrying (C) friendly (D) annoying

7.   He cried with *frustration,* because he had the money and was still prevented from going. *Frustration* (p. 114) means (A) pride (B) disappointment (C) joy (D) triumph

8.   Some people feel *contempt* for those who feel sorry for themselves. *Contempt* (p. 114) means (A) joy (B) anger (C) love (D) disgust

9.   Being afraid when danger is near is a feeling that is *universal. Universal* (p. 115) means (A) unwanted (B) bad (C) found everywhere (D) special

10.   Last winter the flu was very *contagious.* Almost everyone in the class became sick. *Contagious* (p. 115) means (A) dead (B) spreading from person to person (C) usually illegal (D) dangerous

Understanding the Story

Choosing Another Title

1. Which title tells most about the story?
    (A) The End of a City (B) One Person's Courage
    (C) How Wars Start (D) The Joy of Living

Finding Details

2. A tragedy happened right after Jackie McGowan
    left his family off in front of the
    (A) church (B) police station (C) library
    (D) supermarket
3. According to the story, the bombings are a result
    of a bitter struggle between
    (A) the church and the people (B) the government
    and the police (C) people that belong to two
    different religions (D) business and labor
4. Frank was exposed to danger each day because he
    (A) was a police officer (B) drove to work through
    a dangerous area (C) fought in the civil war
    (D) saved people who were injured
5. As Annie came out of the church, she saw a
    (A) group of people talking in the street
    (B) woman pushing a shopping cart (C) boy
    pushed off his bicycle (D) soldier walking with a
    little boy
6. The machine-gun fire came from
    (A) the porch of the church (B) a parked car
    (C) an apartment window (D) the town square
7. After the shooting, the first thing Annie did was
    to run into the square and (A) hide
    (B) call for help (C) say a prayer (D) throw a stone

8. Annie's action resulted in the forming of a
   (A) hospital (B) peace movement (C) new
   government (D) police force

Using Your Reason

9. After the police officer took the child from Annie,
   the story says that Annie "... knew what she
   must do." This means that Annie wanted to
   (A) leave Ireland (B) start a peace movement
   (C) get revenge (D) become a nurse
10. The women threw rocks at Annie because they
    thought she was
    (A) the person who had fired the machine gun
    (B) sympathetic to British soldiers
    (C) a member of the British military
    (D) a reporter

You Be the Judge

1. In our own time several important mass
   movements—anti-Viet Nam war, Civil Rights,
   Women's Liberation—have started as the result of
   the activities of individuals or small groups. What
   movements, if any, have you supported? What
   were your reasons for doing so?
2. People react to a bad situation in different ways.
   Some react by saying, "It's always been this way.
   There's nothing I can do about it." Other people
   react by taking action of some kind. How do you
   react to a bad situation? Give an example.

118

Things To Do

1. Using information found in the library, such as encyclopedias, newspapers, and magazines, trace the beginnings of an important religious, political, or other social movement. Who started it? What difficulties were encountered? Did the movement succeed? How?
2. Look up Ireland in an encyclopedia or other reference book. Read its history and find out what happened that led up to the present situation.

The Lesson
I'll Never Forget

Edna Wilson Warren

Mr. Whigham (I don't recall his first name) was primarily a coach, but he taught ninth-grade civics in his "free period." He had curly hair, a tiny whirlpool of a dimple high on his right cheek and a dimple to match it highlighting the left edge of his smile, which was slow and rare and wonderful.

I was one of the many 14-year-olds who mooned in class and one of the few who tried to get his attention by fair means instead of foul. In algebra I made D's gladly, and C's and B's in other subjects, but I knew more about civics than the writers of the textbook.

A glory-moment came one afternoon after school as I walked along shelling and munching roasted peanuts. I heard footsteps behind me, and a beloved voice said, "Edna, wait for me. I'm going downtown and, if you don't mind, I'll walk along with you."

It was Mr. Whigham! I had a hard time keeping my feet moving with dignity and poise while my heart did crazy flips, and I wanted to skip every step or two. I managed to say, "Have some peanuts?" He took one, and we had a pleasant conversation all the six blocks to town.

When we received reports at school the next week, I stared at mine in consternation: "English B; Algebra D;

REPORT CARD | B
English | D
Algebra | C
Science | F
Civics | B

Science C; *Civics F!*" Then a thought entered my dreaming little head and I smiled. It was possibly an error made on purpose, and maybe Mr. Whigham was also thrilled at the prospect of my seeing him about it after school. There was no question about my A-plus average in civics.

I waited for the other students to clear out and then went to his room. "Have a seat, Edna," he said with that slow smile. I sat at a desk and smiled back.

"You made a mistake on my report card, Mr. Whigham," I said finally.

"Oh, I'm sorry," he said. "May I see it?" He looked it over and then asked, "Where's the error?"

"I know you're teasing," I said brightly. "You know I always make A-plus in civics."

"Oh, no," he said. "You didn't learn that last unit at all, Edna. Let's see . . . what's its title?"

"Keeping Your Town Clean," I answered quickly. "I made a hundred on the test. I also wrote the themes and got my notebook in."

"But you didn't learn it," he persisted.

Fear edged into my voice. "You don't think I *cheated*, do you? Why I—I'm too stubborn to cheat—"

"No, I know you didn't cheat. But you just didn't learn this unit about keeping your town clean."

I stared at him, utterly confused. Although I was near tears, Mr. Whigham did not give an inch.

"Edna," he said quietly, "when I walked to town with you the other day, you offered me peanuts. I ate one and put the shell in my pocket, but you ate peanuts the whole six blocks to town, scattering shells and husks all the way. Finally, you threw the empty bag on the courthouse lawn, and you never *knew* you were adding filth to your town."

I stared into his eyes with a growing comprehension. "Remember, Edna," he added, "never say you've learned something *until it makes a change in your life.*"

The Lesson I'll Never Forget

Building Your Vocabulary

1. Daren's red hair *highlighted* his bright blue eyes and tan complexion. *Highlighted* (p. 121) means (A) hid (B) hurt (C) emphasized (D) changed
2. Although unprepared, Joanne walked out on the stage with *poise* and began to speak. *Poise* (p. 121) means (A) sadness (B) intelligence (C) speed (D) self-confidence
3. Some students feel *consternation* when they receive poor marks on their report cards. *Consternation* (p. 121) means (A) happiness (B) dismay and confusion (C) hungry (D) enthusiasm
4. Before you boil fresh corn, you must strip off the *husks*. *Husks* (p. 123) are (A) fruits (B) grains (C) outer coverings (D) inner cores
5. By the end of the term, the civics class had a *comprehension* of how government works. *Comprehension* (p.123) means (A) understanding (B) dislike (C) experience (D) library

Understanding the Story

Choosing Another Title

1. Which title tells most about the story? (A) Teachers Can Be Trusted (B) To Make a Mistake Is Human (C) Cleanliness Is Next to Godliness (D) Why a Student Failed Civics

Finding Details

2. Mr. Whigham was hired mainly to

124

(A) teach civics (B) serve as a guidance counselor
(C) teach English (D) coach sports
3. When the teacher offered to walk Edna
downtown, she was (A) thrilled (B) offended
(C) eager for everyone to know
(D) too timid to say, "Yes"
4. When Edna saw her civics mark, which of the
following thoughts probably DIDN'T cross her
mind: (A) "He hates me." (B) "It was a mistake."
(C) "He likes me." (D) "I've got to talk with him."
5. The invitation to walk downtown came from
(A) Edna (B) Mr. Whigham (C) the English
teacher (D) a young friend of Edna's
6. For the unit "Keeping Your Town Clean," Edna
had (A) failed the test (B) gotten 100% on the test
(C) failed to turn in the notebook
(D) turned in the notebook late
7. When Edna was about to cry, the teacher
(A) decided to change the mark (B) agreed to give
her another chance (C) remained firm in his
decision (D) requested that the unit be done over
8. The teacher justifies his behavior by telling Edna
that she
(A) is incapable of learning (B) hasn't learned a
lesson unless it makes a change in her life
(C) needs to do some work before she can pass
(D) should study after school

Using Your Reason

9. At the end of the story, Edna understands that
the teacher gave her an "F" because of
(A) something she did outside the classroom
(B) the kind of language she used
(C) her poor study habits
(D) her lack of interest in the subject

10. The teacher's argument that you haven't learned
    something unless it changes your life is true if
    learning means
    (A) gaining knowledge of a skill
    (B) doing what you know
    (C) understanding a principle
    (D) the ability to perform

You Be the Judge

1. Is it right for a teacher to fail a student because of
   something the student does outside the classroom?
   Explain.
2. Was Mr. Whigham correct in allowing Edna to
   litter without warning her that this might affect
   her mark? Explain.
3. What do you think of a person who is silent when
   somebody else does something, and then later
   criticizes the person. Explain.

Things To Do

1. Put yourself in Edna's place. What arguments
   would you have given to get your mark changed?
   Write down your three best arguments.
2. What kind of person was Mr. Whigham? What
   kind of person was Edna? Make a list of words to
   describe Mr. Whigham and a list of words to
   describe Edna.

The Ballad of Reading Gaol

Oscar Wilde

I know not whether laws be right,
  Or whether laws be wrong;
All that we know who lie in jail
  Is that the wall is strong;
And that each day is like a year,
  A year whose days are long.

But this I know, that every law
  That men have made for man,
Since first man took his brother's life,
  And the sad world began,
But straws the wheat and saves the chaff
  With a most evil fan.

This too I know—and wise it were
  If each could know the same—
That every prison that men build
  Is built with bricks of shame,
And bound with bars lest Christ should see
  How men their brothers maim.

With bars they blur the gracious moon,
  And blind the goodly sun;
And they do well to hide their hell,
  For in it things are done
That Son of God nor son of man
  Ever should look upon!

The vilest deeds like poison weeds
  Bloom well in prison air;
It is only what is good in man
  That wastes and withers there.
Pale Anguish keeps the heavy gate,
  And the warder is Despair.

Jesse Jackson
Speaks Out

Jesse Jackson

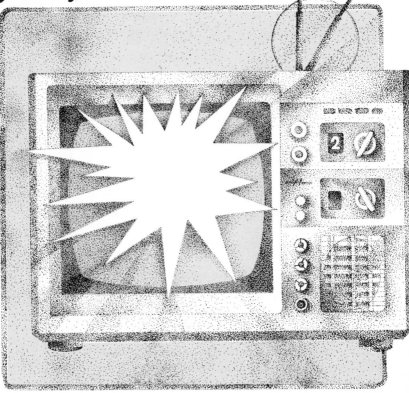

*The Reverend Jesse Jackson is direc-
tor of Operation PUSH (People
United to Save Humanity), a na-
tional organization devoted to the
improvement of life for all poor people. He spends a lot of time talking to
students. He advises them on how
they can become excellent at what
they want to do. He calls this his
"push for excellence" campaign. He
was asked whether he thought radio
and TV helped or hurt people who
are working to achieve excellence.
The following reveals his attitude.
Do you agree or disagree with him?*

Radio and TV hurt because they take too much of our
children's time. Did you know that by the time they're 17
years old, they have watched 18,000 hours of TV? And
they have listened for even more hours on their radios. So
it is very clear that radio and TV have a very great influence on young people. This influence is even greater, in
my opinion, than the influence of parent, teacher or
preacher.

The people who own and run radio and TV stations
should be more careful about the kinds of programs they
produce. If these programs were as worthwhile as a parent's advice, a teacher's lesson or a preacher's sermon, I
would have no quarrel with radio or TV. The trouble is
that station owners are very often not as responsible as
parents, teachers or preachers. So we get altogether too
many programs with the wrong messages. And that both-
ers me.

For example, TV is very big on showing violence. And
all too often it is violence that makes no sense at all. I can
understand violence to defend yourself against someone

who wants to hurt or kill you. But I can't understand violence for the sake of violence. It's that kind of violence that we see and hear so much on TV and radio.

What do we learn from such scenes of senseless violence? All we learn is how to get good at killing people. That's wrong! Parents, teachers and preachers try as hard as they can to undo the damage that these shows create. They are not always successful, because they cannot reach the children's minds the way radio and TV do.

Take for another example the language of dope and sex that we hear on radio and TV. It's especially bad in certain songs which tell young people they can't belong to the "In" crowd unless they get high or engage in sex.

Young people need adults they can model themselves after. Very often the adults they try to imitate are the actors, actresses and singers they see and hear on TV and radio. These are the heroes and the heroines of the young. These are the men and women who have the power to affect the life of those who watch and listen to them all those hours each day and night. Because of this, it's im-

portant for the adult "heroes and heroines" to take responsibility for what they say, what they sing, what they do. They surely must know that they are the models that young people strive to imitate.

Building Your Vocabulary

1. Tad was an *excellent* swimmer and easily won the trophy. *Excellent* (p. 129) means (A) slow (B) careful (C) superior (D) junior

2. Mary was president of her club and was able to use her *influence* to get free movie passes. *Influence* (p. 129) means (A) power (B) money (C) charm (D) parents

3. The *programs* for the holidays include picnics, fireworks, games, and races. *Programs* (p. 129) are
   (A) fields (B) plans (C) sites (D) costs
4. Their *senseless* behavior will not get them what they say they want. *Senseless* (p. 130) means
   (A) determined (B) steady (C) honest (D) foolish
5. Beth wanted to be a cowgirl and took as her *model* Dale Evans. A *model* (p. 131) is a person who is
   (A) imitated (B) talkative (C) active (D) good

Understanding the Story

Choosing Another Title

1. Which title tells most about the story?
   (A) The Preacher Condemns Radio and TV
   (B) The Preacher Tells Something About Himself
   (C) The Preacher Shows How To Be Happy
   (D) The Preacher Gives Three Rules To Live By

Finding Details

2. Jesse Jackson says that by the time they are 17 years old, people have watched
   (A) 5,000 hours of TV (B) 10,000 hours of TV
   (C) 16,000 hours of TV (D) 18,000 hours of TV
3. Jesse Jackson believes that compared with the influence of parents, the influence of TV is
   (A) much less (B) about the same (C) a little less
   (D) greater
4. Jesse Jackson is against showing violence that is
   (A) funny (B) senseless (C) heroic (D) in the line of duty

132

5. Jesse Jackson says he understands violence if it is (A) in self-defense (B) against the military (C) to teach someone a lesson (D) done with humility

Using Your Reason

6. Jesse Jackson's argument would be improved if he told
    (A) what he thinks is wrong with TV and radio
    (B) what his idea of "right messages" on TV would be
    (C) how much time people spend watching TV
    (D) his opinion about dope and sex
7. Which of the following questions represents the strongest argument of a person who DISAGREES with Jesse Jackson's approach:
    (A) What group of people should have the power to control what goes on public air waves?
    (B) Aren't the "heroes and heroines" of TV already responsible?
    (C) Do parents, teachers, and preachers really want to control children's minds?
    (D) Why should people who run TV and radio stations be careful?

You Be the Judge

1. The Constitution of the United States says in the Bill of Rights that "Congress shall make no law ... abridging the freedom of speech, or of the press. ..." Do you think it is a good idea for people to be allowed to say what they want to on TV or radio? Explain.

133

2. Someone has said, "No person or group of persons is 'good enough' to be entrusted with the power to censor what other people read, look at, or hear. Given power, people will ultimately use it to increase their own power at the expense of the common good." Do you agree with this statement? Disagree? Explain.

3. What do you think people should do if they don't like what they see or hear on radio or TV? Explain.

4. Jesse Jackson says that on radio and TV there are "too many programs with wrong messages." Would you like it if Jesse Jackson had the power to prevent you from listening to records, shows, or programs that have what he thinks are "wrong messages"? Why? Explain.

5. Jesse Jackson thinks that radio and TV hurt people who are "struggling to achieve excellence." Do you think you are hurt or helped by what you see or hear on radio and TV? Explain.

Things To Do

1. Ask your friends and classmates how much time they spend watching TV. Try to figure out how many hours and days in a month it amounts to for the average teenager.

2. Find out the kinds of programs your friends watch on TV. Find out which are their favorite programs. Do these programs have a lot of violence? Do you think violence helps or hurts a show's popularity? Explain.

3. Who are your favorite performers on TV or the radio? Do you model yourself after them in any way? How? Do you feel they are a good or bad influence? Explain.

They Grind
Exceeding Small

Ben Ames Williams

This story was written over 60 years ago. It shows something of how hard life was in a country town that might have been in some part of the United States. What is really important, though, is that the story tells about the harshness of one particular man. It indicates the kind of trouble this man caused others. And it also shows how he himself was made to suffer.

The title of the story is taken from a verse by the German poet Friedrich von Logau (1604–1655). The line that it is taken from reads, "Though the mills of God grind slowly, yet they grind exceeding small." When you read this story, you will see how that is true at least in one case.

Hazen Kinch was a miser. He was mean, tight, cruel, and hateful. When he laughed, which was not often, what came out was a cackle. The people of the town feared and hated him. When he loaned them money, they never got out of debt. His wife feared and hated him. He had taken her because her father could not pay his debts. The mare that pulled his sleigh feared and hated him. Hazen beat her every chance he got. And yet Hazen seemed to get on in the world. He owned more property and had more money than anyone around. He pleased nobody, and nothing seemed to please him except his little son.

The boy, not quite two years old, was the apple of Hazen's eye. The baby was not healthy. He had a deformed leg. His eyes seemed filled with hatred and fear. Yet Hazen loved him. If Hazen could love anything. Whenever the child's mother moved near him, the baby bawled.

"Leave him alone," Hazen would command. "Stand away!"

137

I was the only one who was not afraid of Hazen Kinch. I owed him nothing. And perhaps because of this, I was the only one to whom he would speak in a half-way friendly manner.

One winter day Hazen and I were to drive into town. When I got to his house, he was hitching his mare to the sleigh. She rolled her eyes backwards at him and pulled her head away.

"Do you think we ought to go?" I asked. "It is going to snow."

Hazen laughed his little cackle. "How do you know?"

"The clouds," I said. "And it's getting warmer."

"I'll not have it snowing," he snapped. "I just won't have it."

Just before we left, Hazen went into the house. He picked up his little son. He was almost tender with him. He turned to me.

"It's a fine boy," he said.

Then he turned to his wife. "Take good care of him," he ordered. "I'll be back."

Then we went out to the sleigh and bundled ourselves up against the cold. It was a six mile drive into town. Hazen looked up at the sky.

"I'll not have it snowing," he growled.

But even as he said it, the snow began to come down. The wind howled. The wet snow hit our faces and stung our eyes. Suddenly we ran into a snow drift across the road. The mare broke through bravely. But the sleigh leaned to one side. Hazen and I were thrown out into the deep snow. I was not hurt and neither was Hazen. He got up and brushed the snow off his coat. Then he walked over to the mare. He reached up and pulled her head down. He grabbed one of her ears and gave a hard tug. The mare snorted in pain. Then he took his whip and gave her a cruel cut across the knee.

"No horse throws me out into the snow," Hazen muttered.

Then, in silence, we got back into the sleigh. Slowly, and in great pain, the mare pulled us into town.

Once we got to town I went to Hazen Kinch's office with him. Because of the snow we would have to stay in town overnight. We would sleep in Hazen's office. He would not pay for a hotel room. Hazen tried to phone his house to find out how his son was. But the lines were down, and he could not get through.

"That's a fine boy," said Hazen Kinch. "He'll make a good man—like his father." And he gave that hateful chuckle.

Late in the afternoon the door of Hazen's office opened. There stood Doan Marshey. He was a terribly thin little man. His eyes were sad looking. His mustache was sad looking. All of Marshey was very sad looking. He stood sadly in the doorway.

"Come in! Come in!" snapped Hazen. "Don't waste all my heat."

Marshey shuffled in and took off his snowy gloves.

139

"What's your business, Marshey?" said Hazen. "Your interest is due."

"I know, Mr. Kinch," Marshey said. "But I can't pay it all."

"You never can pay," snorted Hazen. "How much do you have?"

"Eleven dollars and fifty cents," said Doan.

"You owe me twenty dollars."

"I aim to pay it when the hens begin to lay their eggs."

Hazen laughed that nasty cackle. "You always aim to pay, Marshey. If your old farm was worth anything, I'd put you out in this snow."

"Please don't do that, Mr. Kinch. I aim to pay," pleaded Marshey.

"Well," said Hazen, "give me what you've got."

Marshey reached into his jacket pocket. His hands were trembling with cold. He took out a little cloth pouch. Out of this he took two quarters. Then he began opening a little roll of bills. I saw something drop from the pouch onto the table. It looked like a dollar bill. I was about to say something. But Hazen reached his hand out like a cat's paw. He covered the bill with his hand. When he took his hand back, the bill was gone.

Then Hazen counted out the money Marshey gave him.

"All right, Marshey. Eleven dollars and fifty cents. I'll give you a receipt. But remember. Have the rest of the money before the end of the month. Or out you go!"

Marshey looked very tired. "That's all I have now, Mr. Kinch. But I'll get the rest."

Then he walked to the door. "Thank you, sir," he muttered very humbly. And he shuffled out.

I was very curious.

"What was that you picked up from the table, Hazen," I asked.

He opened his hand. It was a crumpled, dirty dollar bill.

140

"That's Marshey's," I said. "Aren't you going to give it back to him?"

"No!" Hazen cackled. "If he can't take care of his money, I can. Anyway, he still owes me."

Just then we heard Marshey's tired steps outside the door. He came in slowly and sadly.

"Mr. Kinch," he said, "I think I lost a dollar. Did I drop it in here?"

"No," said Hazen. "I thought you said you gave me all you had."

"Well, it wasn't mine really," said Marshey. "It was to get some medicine for somebody."

"Well, it's not here. Maybe you dropped it in the snow," said Hazen.

When Marshey turned to go, I looked at Hazen's face. He was laughing silently and cruelly.

The next morning came bright and sunny. It was still cold, and the snow was thick on the ground. Hazen Kinch hitched up the mare, and we got into the sleigh.

"I can't wait to see my boy," said Hazen. "He's a really fine boy, that one."

On the ride back I was silent. I kept thinking about Hazen and his meanness. How could a man be so harsh? How could he frighten so many people so badly. Above all, I wondered, how could he keep getting away with it? Would he ever be caught and punished for his cruelty to others? For his lying? And if so, what would his punishment be? I watched him out of the corner of my eye. He seemed as calm and content as a man could be. It was clear to see that he was perfectly happy. It was his world. All men and women were his slaves.

When we got to Hazen's house, there was no smoke coming from the chimney. The house looked strangely quiet.

"She's let the fire go out again," snarled Hazen. "Wait till I get hold of her."

We clambered down from the sleigh and stumbled into the house. When we got in, Hazen's wife was sitting on the bed in the corner of the big kitchen. She got up. For the first time I saw that there was no fear in her eyes. She looked Hazen straight in the eye.

"I'm home, woman," Hazen rasped. "Where's the boy?"

There was silence for a moment. Then his wife spoke, almost as though she was dreaming.

"The boy? He's dead!"

The silence was awful. I looked at Hazen Kinch. His face was very white and very still. A muscle in one cheek twitched and jerked. The blood drained from his face. He became white as death itself.

"Where is he?"

The woman pointed over her shoulder with her chin.

On the bed, twisted and terrible, lay the little, pitiful body.

"I did all I could," she whispered. "He had a bad cough. Remember I asked you to get some medicine. You said no need. You said he's a fine boy. So when it became bad, I went over to Doan Marshey. I gave him a dollar to buy the medicine."

"Why didn't he buy it, then?" Hazen almost squeaked.

"When he came back, he told me he lost the money. He said he lost it in your office. He's sure he lost it there."

The silence became deadly. Then Hazen leaned back like a man being broken. His face was terrible to see. His mouth opened wide.

He screamed.

I knew then that when man does not punish, God does.

Building Your Vocabulary

1. Hazen Kinch hitched the horse to the *sleigh*. A *sleigh* (p. 137) is a
   (A) saddle (B) harness (C) vehicle (D) railing
2. The expression *"apple of Hazen's eye"* (p. 137) means that the child was
   (A) adored by Hazen (B) watched over constantly by Hazen (C) often beaten by Hazen (D) ruled sternly by Hazen
3. Marshey kept his money in a little *pouch*. A *pouch* (p. 140) is a kind of
   (A) drawer (B) box (C) bag (D) belt
4. Hazen Kinch reached his hand out *"like a cat's paw"* (p. 140). This means that he moved his hand very (A) awkwardly (B) quickly (C) leisurely (D) carelessly

5. Marshey *shuffled* out of Kinch's office. *Shuffled* (p. 140) means
(A) moved slowly (B) tripped (C) skipped (D) fell down

Understanding the Story

Choosing Another Title

1. Which title tells most about the story?
(A) Kinch's Wife (B) The Judgment of God (C) The Snowstorm (D) Marshey's Revenge

Finding Details

2. Hazen's mare showed her fear by
(A) kicking him (B) throwing him (C) running away (D) rolling her eyes
3. How did Hazen feel about his son?
(A) Proud (B) Angry (C) Thrilled (D) Unhappy
4. Hazen Kinch's son had difficulty with his
(A) legs (B) chest (C) eyes (D) arms
5. Doan Marshey is described as being
(A) strong (B) sad (C) hairy (D) tall
6. Doan Marshey had an extra dollar in order to buy
(A) cigarettes (B) medicine (C) milk (D) wine
7. How did Hazen Kinch usually feel about himself?
(A) Satisfied (B) Angry (C) Unhappy (D) Doubtful
8. After the boy's death, Hazen Kinch's wife became
(A) humble (B) unafraid (C) happy (D) excited

Using Your Reason

9. According to the story, sometimes God's punishment is

(A) unnoticed (B) too easy (C) slow in coming
(D) too late
10. Hazen's final look showed that he felt
(A) defiance (B) relief (C) disgust (D) agony

You Be the Judge

1. Do you think that people, in their lifetime, are always punished when they are selfish and cruel? Explain.
2. This story suggests that the boy dies because of his father's wickedness. According to the story, the boy didn't do anything wicked. Do you think it is fair that an innocent person suffer because of what a wicked person does? Why do innocent people sometimes suffer?

Things To Do

1. Do you think that the events that happened in this story caused Hazen Kinch to change his way of life? Why? Write a paragraph that begins with one of the following sentences:
   A. I think Hazen Kinch changed for the better. He showed this change by ... B. I think Hazen Kinch remained the same because ... C. I think Hazen Kinch became more cruel and mean. The first thing he did was ...
2. The story says that Hazen loved his son, "if Hazen could love anything." This suggests that maybe Hazen didn't love his son. For instance, perhaps Hazen simply regarded his son as property. He was upset at the end of the story because his property had been taken away. What do you think?

Write a paragraph that begins with one of the following sentences:

A.   I think Hazen really loved his son because . . .

B.   I don't think Hazen really loved his son because . . .